A Journey Through Suicide Valley

Author

Dr.Deepthi Balla

B.Sc.,M.Ed., M.A.(Psy), PhD

Published by : Self-Published

Address

Dr.Deepthi Balla

Seethammadhara

Visakhapatnam

Andhra Pradesh

Printed by

VISAKHA OFFSET PRINTERS

48-13-8, Flat No.1, Old Siticable Building, Janakirama Street, Srinagar, Visakhapatnam - 530016. Ph : 8099228855

ISBN-978-93-5419-822-9

Printed in December, 2020
Coverpage Photo by Fabrizio Conti on upsplash
Coverpage Designed by Visakha Offset Printers,
Visakhapatnam, Andhra Pradesh, India.

Disclaimer

This book, "A Journey through Suicide Valley" is a Nonfiction compilation of information regarding suicide which is taken from several textbooks, journals and online resources. This book is composed in the form of a dialogue with the readers. I put forward my passionate insights into how suicidal behaviour develops. I request the readers to follow the links given in the book to further their knowledge about suicidal behaviour.

I strictly request the readers not to use the pictures given in the book without the consent from the original contributors. I took permission from them to use it for the edification of the public regarding suicide. I honour these researchers for their extensive work on suicide. Thus I implore the readers to benefit from their work by gaining an understanding of suicide. But do not use them without their permission. It will be considered violating their copyright policies.

Finally I want the readers to know that this book is for enhancing your knowledge about suicide. It is not a self-help book. Through the reading of this book you will gain proper understanding of suicide and will be aware of identifying suicidal behaviour. If you identify any of the symptoms suggested in the book in yourself or your beloved or relatives, friends, I suggest that you would take the help of clinical professionals like mental health doctors.

Author
Dr Deepthi Balla
B.Sc., M.Ed., M.A.(Psy), Ph.D

Preface

Prevention is Better than Cure. We all know it but could never reflect on it unless we get some Physical ailment. Similarly, our Mental health problems though seem manageable or negligible need a lot of attention as prevention is the main source of healing. Suicide now considered as a mental health problem needs awareness among the public as we cannot identify every suicidal person in a large community. Though ignorance is considered bliss, here ignorance costs the lives of our loved ones. This book is prepared with the sole aim of educating the readers who can take assertive steps in identifying the suicidal thoughts among his beloved and do the needful.

When I joined my PhD in 2010, the topic that I was passionate about is "depression among adolescents." I wanted to research this area since 2007. I am so interested in it as it deals with identifying the sources which inhibit an individual to perform with his or her actual potential. It is the most significant factor to be considered behind suicides. I found that depression is the strong predictor of suicidal ideation and if it is not diagnosed at earlier stages (by 17 or 18 years of age) would lead to suicidal attempts (David Fergusson et al., 2005).

I also found the article where the report of NCRB stated like this :

"Every four-minute, one person takes his or her life in the country and one in each three of victims is a youth below the age of 30 years, the latest report of National Crime Records Bureau

(NCRB) has revealed. ("Economic Times, 2011, Jan 16)"

So I showed it to my research guide and then started working with the thesis. But my thesis results showed that amongst 14-19 years there were 229 students (amongst 1013students) who were thinking about suicide but cannot say about whether will commit or not. The reason expressed by them was that they feel that they are obligated to study for their parents' wishes. So educating parents was imperative. But immediately after my PhD was finished a professor and a Psychiatrist notified me that irrespective of different programs being conducted (very few programs) at schools, gathering parents, there is a big hurdle of motivating them. It is difficult due to their work schedules and attitudes. There are a couple of debates on this issue but no use, according to them.

Meanwhile another report by WHO was alarming.

According to the World Health Organization Report, "an Indian commits suicide every two minutes. ("Bagla Pallava , September 04, 2014 20:28 IST)

According to NITI central news, WHO reported that "in number of suicides, India accounts for nearly a third of the global total and more than twice as many in China, which is second on the list. There is high rate of suicide among young people, aged between 15 to 29 years." (Niticentral, Sep 07, 2014).

> *"63 per cent of all suicides reported in India were in the 15-39 age group........37 per cent of global suicide among women and 34 per cent of men in 2016."* (The Week, New Delhi September 24, 2018, 15:50 IST)

So after observing these reports and the initiatives made by the government to decriminalize suicide attempts (Hindustan Times, New Delhi, Jun 01, 2018, 23:51 IST), I felt amazed why such attempts were still heard in our Country India and all its 29 states.

But most alarming incidents which compelled me to produce this book as fast as possible are suicides of celebrities, which are mostly attributed to their depression. This needs closure. Not all depressed commit suicide. The reasons behind them or the factors that lead them to take such drastic steps must be understood before making such interpretations.

So with this short book, I am going to describe the what, why and how of "suicide". After reading this, I hope all of us at our homes can identify whether our family members had suicidal tendencies so that help is sought at the right time.

Acknowledgement

I thank Almighty God first that he motivated me to write this book and also for enabling me to give the title of the book as "A Journey through Suicide Valley."

Next, I am grateful to all the researchers who have provided their full-text articles to read and permitted me to use these.

In particular, I am thankful to Karen Wetherall, Research associate, University of Glasgow, working under respected Professor, Dr Rory C O'Connor, Head of Suicide Behaviour Research Lab. He propounded the theory of IMV model, which is the most significant of theories in the field of suicide research. She asked him for permission to use this article in my book, with their permission I used the corresponding pictures in this book. In this regard, Derek Paul De Beurs, Ph.D., provided me with further 'in-press' pictures.

I am extremely thankful to José Manoel Bertolote, Professor, Griffith University, Brisbane, Australia, Australian Institute for Suicide Research and Prevention who outrightly permitted me to reuse the figures of his article.

Giorgio Falgares, Professor (Associate), University of Palermo, Department of Psychology Educational Science and Human Movement, who kindly provided me additional information on this topic, which is found to be so useful in the compilation of the material in this book.

I am also thankful to Béatrice Marianne Ewalds-Kvist, Associate professor, Department of Psychology, Stockholm University, Stockholm, Sweden, who provided me case article on logotherapy and gave some suggestions regarding this.

Here are the other researchers who came forward to provide their articles for the compilation of the book. I thank each of these for their generosity.

Massimiliano Orri, Postdoctoral research fellow, McGill University, Montréal, Canada, McGill Group for Suicide Studies - Department of Psychiatry

☞ Jeffrey S. Ashby, Georgia State University, Atlanta, United States, Department of Counseling and Psychological Services

☞ Nobuyuki Mitsui, Professor (Assistant), Hokkaido University, Sapporo, Japan, Department of Psychiatry

☞ Rui C Campos, Professor (Associate) and Research chair, Universidade de Évora, Évora, Portugal, Department of Psychology - School of Social Sciences and CIEP-UE

☞ Jill M Hooley, Professor of Psychology and Area Head, Clinical Program, Harvard University, Cambridge, United States, Department of Psychology

☞ Kounseok Lee, Clinical Assistant Professor, Hanyang University Medical Center, Seoul, South Korea, Department of Psychiatry

☞ Suhail A. Doi, Qatar University, Doha, Qatar, Department of Population Medicine, College of Medicine

☞ S. Ogawa, Nagasaki University, Nagasaki, Japan, Center for Health and Community Medicine

☞ Anna Szucs, Centro de Pesquisa Mokiti Okada, São Paulo, Brazil, Department of Neurology

☞ Raffaella Calati, Non tenure track researcher (type A Italian system), Università degli Studi di Milano-Bicocca, Italy

☞ Imke Baetens, Assistant Professor at the Vrije Universiteit Brussel (Belgium)

☞ Susanne Hörz-Sagstetter, Professor of Clinical Psychology and Psychotherapy, Psychologische Hochschule Berlin, Germany

☞ Ivo Krejci, Professor, University of Geneva, Switzerland

☞ Cen Wang, Adjunct Senior Research Fellow, Charles Sturt University, Bathurst, Australia, School of Teacher Education

☞ Aaron Pincus, Professor of Psychology, Pennsylvania State University, University Park, United States, Department of Psychology

☞ Joana Duarte, Research Assistant, Malmö University, Malmö, Sweden, Department of Urban Studies (US)

☞ Regina Miranda, Professor, City University of New York - Hunter College, Manhattan, United States, Department of Psychology

☞ Sanea Mihaljevi?, Medical Doctor, General Hospital Virovitica, Croatia, Virovitica, Psychiatry department

☞ Delishia M. Pittman, Professor (Assistant), George Washington University, Washington, D.C., United States, Department of Counseling and Human Development

☞ Yu-Hsin Huang, attending physician, Mackay Memorial Hospital, Taipei, Taiwan, Department of Psychiatry

About the Book

To live in this world as a human is a privilege. One can touch and experience the natural resources while utilizing the in-built high-level cognitive functions to the use these resources on earth productively for the benefit of fellow humans and lower life forms. Humans are the only ones on this planet who can kill both animals and fellow humans alike. Ironically, at the same time, humans kill themselves feeling handicapped of facing life's situations. In comparison to animals co-existing on this world with us, we do have a high level of comprehending abilities, communication power, problem-solving and creative powers. Then raises the question of why do humans commit suicide. In this book, I am trying to give an analytical view of the perspectives of suicide victims. It seems that suicidal individuals lack the self-confidence to live in this world by facing the reality. Is this true? If so, it amazes me to find that -when they have the confidence to kill themselves, why couldn't they use the same confidence to live? In another perspective, they took a strong decision to kill themselves. That strong will power could have led to the resolution to live in this world. So why are they lacking the confidence to live in this world? Throughout this book, I am going to research the issues concerned with why a person falls into the depths of despair and pit of suicide attempt and try to reflect upon interventions that are available in the world today to help fellow humans who are thinking of making a big decision of taking their lives.

So the title will be "A Journey through Suicide Valley". Valley is two types -one where everything is fertile (e.g., Indus valley civilization) and the other type of valley is with darkness, gloom. So, I aim to talk about the issues of a traveller, who is suicidal, wandering with a heavy heart in the valley of darkness, which is filled with suicidal thoughts.   Imagine that there is a companion with a suicidal person, who is walking along with him in the suicide valley and this companion understands his pains, suffering and emotional cry. How good will it feel to the suicidal person that someone understands him? This book is not sympathetic or supportive to a suicidal person, but through empathetic support, aims to be a companion to all who are exhibiting suicidal behaviour and their beloved.

- Dr Deepthi Balla
B.Sc., M.Ed., M.A., (Psy), Ph.D

A Journey through Suicide Valley

INDEX

		Page No.
Chapter 1	Preparation for the journey	1-15
Chapter 2	The Lone Traveler	16-54
Chapter 3	The Path	55-81
Chapter 4	The Crossroads	82-90
Chapter 5	The High Way	91-104

A Journey through Suicide Valley

Chapter 1

The Preparation for the Journey

In many philosophical texts, it is written that those who are born have to die one day. We are born alone and we go alone. But the concept often forgotten is we are born with the combination of X and Y chromosomes. I mean to say is that -our birth is not a lonely process. The entire body of our mother and the cells in her body are in continuous support to develop us as a fetus with help of father's genes. So we are not alone when we are in the womb, growing up (friends, relatives, colleagues) and we are not alone by the time we become old (if you do not terminate it in the middle of a lifetime), we are productive at least in one of the areas of life like -to have children, did some work which might have positively influenced someone else's life. So in the memories and the actual living space of individuals, we exist. When we are sharing others life completely (life partner) or partially (children and grandchildren) we are not alone.

With this said, I am asking for all those who might be thinking about suicide to give me a chance to edify us (all) and also those who consider suicidal people as insane or ill, a chance to provide a clear and reflective idea of what suicidal individuals are going through and how magnificently these have endured the struggles so far. I hope sincerely that the reading of this book makes you take courage to move forward to get out of the pit of helplessness and hopelessness.

What is suicide?

Let us take a look at the term "suicide" and what it means from an etymological perspective. I mean to say that I am going to explain how the word came into existence. In the beginning, this word was used in Latin "suicidium. As per the Etymological practice, the word is the combination of two words "sui" (self) and Cidium (to slay). It infers that "self-killing".

Suicide (n.)

> *"deliberate killing of oneself," 1650s, from Modern Latin suicidium "suicide," from Latin sui "of oneself" (genitive of se "self"), from PIE *s(u)w-o- "one's own," from root *s(w)e- (see idiom) + -cidium "a killing," from caedere "to slay" (from PIE root *kae-id- "to strike").*

Retrieved from https://www.etymonline.com/word/suicide

The above definition includes other terminology making the meaning more confused. But I retained it to show the actual intent behind the naming of the term. We do not have any objections with "su" but with "cidium", similar meaning inferring words such as "caedere (to slay)" and "Kae-id ("to strike"- cutting off the tree from the root). Combining similar words, it can be inferred that suicide is a deliberate and authoritative act of an individual to forcefully end one's life as if striking a tree from its roots. It also gives a sense of the rage of the suicidal individual at the time of taking one's life. " I will kill myself which is the best solution **one's and for all.**" Eradication (destruction) of life seems to be the only solution for the suicidal individual for the crisis he or she feels at that time. This has a similar notion to the views of Antoon A. Leenaars (2010), who pointed out the psychological definition of suicide as provided by the father of Suicidology, Edwin Shneider, in his book on "definition of suicide". That is

"Currently in the Western world, suicide is a conscious act of self-induced annihilation, best understood as a multidimensional malaise in a needful individual who defines an issue for which the suicide is perceived as the best solution."

The above definition emphasizes the reason stated by the suicidal person for his violent action. Every suicidal person gives a reason for his unmet need for which he sees it as the only solution.

But the word suicide (a French) became the most commonly used word for this intentional activity.

"Suicide" is a modern concept. In English, the wording did not emerge before the 1650s and in the Romance languages not before the second half of the eighteenth century ("suicide" in French, "suicidio" in Italian). The invention of the latinized term mirrored less stringent criminal prosecution of self-killing, in the wake of harsher punishments and the creation of a statutory offense that had found their semantic expression in the nominalization of "self-murder" since the second half of the sixteenth century (Andreas Bähr, 2013)

The above description showed that the word "suicide" showcased the activity with less criminal punishment. It means that the word during its translation got modification in terms of meaning, which we cannot prove due to non-familiarity with the language and cultural set up of those times at which the name is given to the act.

The study of suicide got its momentum with the influential work of French Sociologist Emile Durkheim (1858-1917), who believed that suicide has social reasons as precipitators. So based on the survey data of then suicide statistics of European countries he wrote a book entitled "Suicide (1897)."

Durkheim through his survey data propagated that there are two forms of suicide. He explained that these two forms are due to extremities in "social integration " and "moral regulation", of the suicidal person in reaction to the society in which he is living. Both of these things are on a continuum means to have two extreme variations. At one extreme of social integration type, the suicidal individuals are too deviant or at another extreme, too close to the social norms. At one extreme of moral regulation type, is individuals expectations (aspirations/needs) from the social variables (family, friends employers etc) and at another extreme is how the social variables affect the individual in a way that he doesn't want it to behave (pressurize).

In the 'social integration type', especially at one end of the polar, he identified that the individual keeps himself away from social integration related issues. For instance, 'social norms, values and support networks enjoyed by most people" but not by this suicidal individual, made him think of suicide. So such a form of suicide is called **"egoistic suicide"**. Durkheim explained that egoistic suicide results from "feelings of self-reproach and sense of failure and more common among single than married people, arises from Social cohesion"(Andrew M.Colman, 2006)

At another extreme of social integration, is observed

among the individuals who are over-compliant and conformed with following social norms, tend to have **"altruistic suicide."** These individuals do not consider their self or needs of oneself and give priority to the society which they are serving. Patriotic people are the best examples of it. We all in one or other occasion of independence days have heard narrations about patriotic people (from our grandparents' reports) who committed suicide in reluctance to submission to the enemy nation's authority. Durkheim states that this form of suicide is

"carried out for the benefit of others and relatively common in Japan, arises from a sense of failure to society." (Andrew Colman, 2006).

It is explained that culture also has a role in suicide acceptance.

"The Japanese regard suicide as an honourable way to take responsibility, similar to seppuku (hara-kiri, self-disembowelment), the traditional form of suicide committed by warriors in the feudal era. (Andrew Cheng, Chau-Shoun Lee, 2000)

In the 'moral regulation' type he identified that economical and social changes culminate suicide among those who are deprived of their basic needs. Thus he named it "anomic suicide".

In an article on "The Study of Suicide by Emile Durkheim", Crossman, Ashley (2018, September 29), explained it clearly. That is as followed.

"Anomic suicide is an extreme response by a person who

experiences anomie, a sense of disconnection from society and a feeling of not belonging resulting from weakened social cohesion. Anomie occurs during periods of serious social, economic, or political upheaval, which result in quick and extreme changes to society and everyday life. In such circumstances, a person might feel so confused and disconnected that they choose to commit suicide."

In an article on "What does Durkheim's study on suicide tell us about the role of social theory in his work more generally?" -Noel Thomas debriefed the further variations of Anomic Suicide as propagated by Durkheim as followed.

"Anomic suicide occurs when there is an imbalance of means and needs (Taylor, 1982; p. 25). Therefore, dramatic changes in economic or social conditions could often act as a precursor to anomic suicide. However, Durkheim went further to draw classifications within anomic suicide itself." (Noel Thomas, n.d).

As further partitions are somewhat hard to understand, I am explaining them in simple terms in the following paragraphs.

Noel Thomas describes that Durkheim further divided Anomic suicide into four subcategories.

1.   Acute economic anomie -caused by social conflicts that are aroused due to reductions in the economical support system of pre-industrialized society. In western and European countries, guilds and religious institutions used to provide monetary regulations and played a major role in money circulation. The ruling of kings and feudal Lords were mostly influenced by religious authorities until industrialization. Policy changes in economy and

governance due to industrialization, lead to decreased dependency on such institutions and so the sudden change in money generation and circulation, brought confusion among the public leading to suicides, which is observed mostly among economically vulnerable people.

2. Chronic economic anomie -the continuity in ambiguity in the public regarding whom to depend on for their economic needs as the previous monetary support systems were then stagnated. Even after the industrial revolution, accumulating money had become difficult. This was expressed as the cause of this type of suicide.

3. Micro social level suicide -*"could come about as a result of sudden change and a consequent inability to adapt, for example widowhood or child bereavement."* Micro-level of any society indicates the individuals who are living in that society. So the negative changes in the lives of people living in it denote this type of suicide.

4. Chronic domestic anomie

"referred to the manner in which the institution of marriage affected suicide rates among women."

Another extreme of moral integration type -"Fatalistic suicide" was beautifully explained by Crossman Ashely (2018, September 29) as followed.

*"**Fatalistic suicide** occurs under conditions of extreme social regulation resulting in oppressive conditions and a denial of the self and of agency. In such a situation a person may elect to die rather than continue enduring the oppressive conditions, such as the case of suicide among prisoners."*

The above paragraph indicates that an individual's tendency to opt for suicide as he is not able to bear the social regulations. These regulations make the individual deny his existence and the social agency both which he believed to be necessary for living. If this agency perceived to be a positive source of support, then it could have been a protective factor against any negative thought and action. But since the individual feels that it too is not a support system to him, he loses hope and with a stroke of a negative event, as it crosses his enduring capacity, would resort to suicide. Fatalistic suicide can be explained in these terms. The agency that is very crucial for being a social support or protective factor is Family. Now think about what a blow it will be on an individual when he feels that his family is against him and none could help him for the pain he is going through.

Figure 1: Durkheim's Description of Suicides

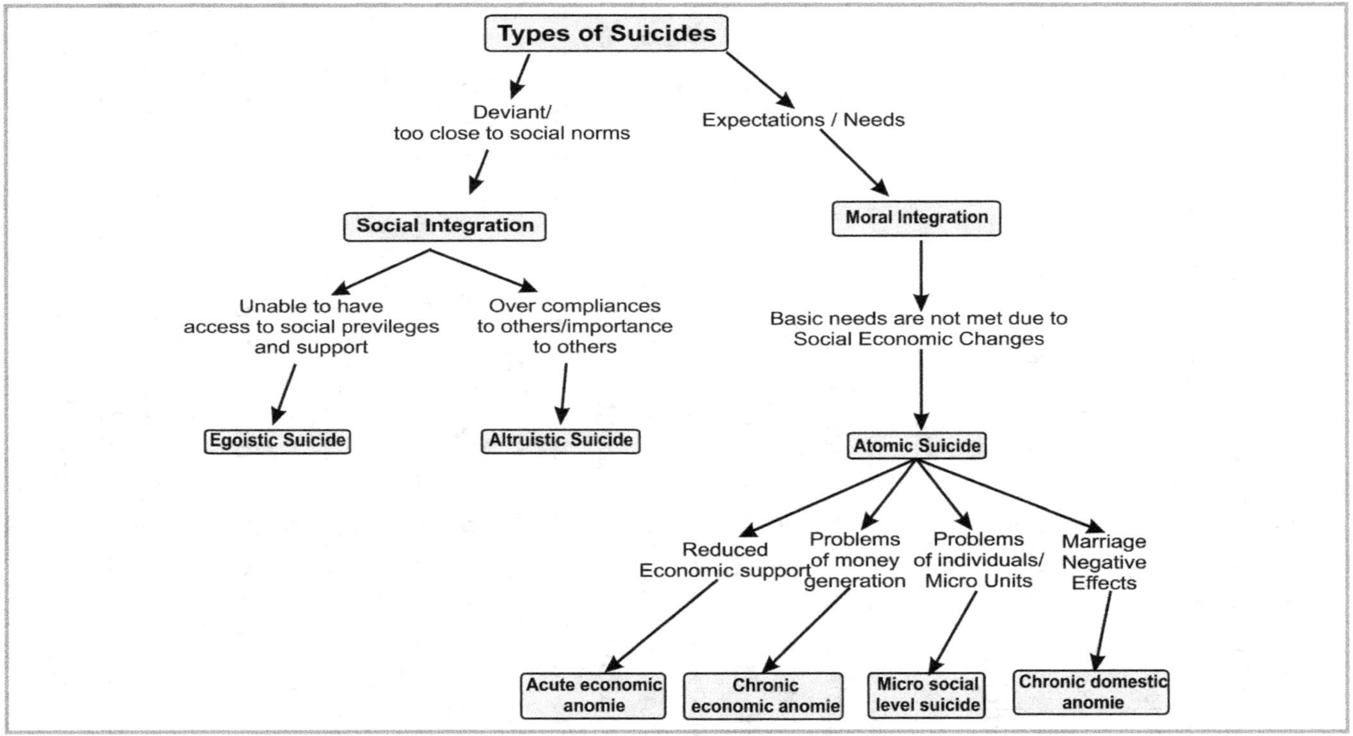

Note: Above figure is created by Dr Deepthi Balla for clarity purpose of the readers

The above types of suicide are defined nearly a century ago but still, show how people today are prone to suicide. For example, farmers' suicide in India is explainable to Anomic suicide.

As we have seen until now the sociological perspective behind suicide, we shall now look at the medical, clinical aspects of suicide.

When someone reports that a person has committed suicide, we took the word lightly but give importance to the probable causes of the suicidal act and mostly view the victim's act from a different angle than what really might have been. Most of the common questions that arise in the observers are as followed. First, the observers just focus on the question of whether he survived the suicide attempt or not. Then their focus shifts to learning about how did he commit suicide, why did he commit suicide etc. Some observers go to the extent of attributing the cause of the death to rumours like failed love affairs, illegal relationships etc. These will harm the family members of the victim. It may in some cases hurt their status and these may resort to suicide later due to these damaging rumours. Thus I implore the readers to have an objective view of the victim's reasons to commit suicide. Once you develop this view, then the burden of suicide upon the family members and neighbours would be lessened. If it develops in a community as a chain reaction, the attitude of a child who might be thinking of suicide could be modified as the child would approach his parents to discuss the issue that is making him think that life is a waste.

So as a first step to achieve this attitudinal change, let us understand the meaning behind the word suicide, then your orientation towards suicide will change.

John Kalafat (2005), described the term suicidality and gave definitions of the concerned terms as followed;

"Suicidality refers to all suicide-related behaviours and thoughts, including completing or attempting suicide, and suicidal ideation."

The less harmful of these which needs careful attention is suicidal ideation. Identifying this makes it easier to predict other forms of suicidality and hence treatment could be sought at the right time.

John Kalafat continued to describe it as …..

"Suicidal ideation consists of thoughts of harming or killing oneself; and, frequency, intensity, and duration are all posited as important to determining the severity of ideation. "

So when we cannot perceive the suicidal ideation in a person, he will manifest them in action, which is 'suicidal attempt' and ironically if it succeeds in death of the committed, is called 'suicide completion.'

Fortunately, Suicidal ideation is perceivable. Many who are working to prevent suicide were conducting large campaigns by forming associations and governing bodies. One such an association in America has provided these signs for public awareness. I suggest you would go to the following link to have more understanding of the suicide-related work they are doing. In every country, at least one organization is dedicated to Suicide.

Table 1: American Association for Suicide Prevention (AFSP) in 2018 provided the following symptoms as

'SUICIDE WARNING SIGNS'

Talk	Behaviour	Mood
Killing themselves	Increased use of alcohol or drugs	Depression
Feeling hopeless	Looking for a way to end their lives, such as searching online for methods	Anxiety
Having no reason to live	Withdrawing from activities	Loss of interest
Being a burden to others	Isolating from family and friends	Irritability
Feeling trapped	Sleeping too much or too little	Humiliation/ Shame
Unbearable pain	Visiting or calling people to say goodbye	Agitation/Anger
	Giving away prized possessions	Relief/Sudden Improvement
	Aggression	
	Fatigue	

The above data are taken from
https://afsp.org/about-suicide/risk-factors-and-warning-signs/

We can do nothing about suicide completion as the person has already lost his life by the time one reaches to the victim. So most of the concern of the clinicians is reducing suicidal behaviour. Clinicians especially psychiatrists are more intended to reduce suicidal behaviour amongst all the mentally ill-health patients. It is to be noted that in most of the mentally ill-health conditions, suicide behaviour is one of the prominent symptoms to consider for severe treatment procedures like Electro Convulsion Therapy (shock treatment). So for the accuracy of the diagnosis of the symptoms denoting suicidal behaviour, all of the Psychiatrists and even clinical psychologists look at the most rigorous compilation of mental disorders by thousands of clinicians over the world, that is - WHO's International Classification of Disorders-10. (ICD_10) But almost of similar value is the Diagnostic and Statistical Manual of Mental Disorders, Fifth Edition (DSM-5) of the American Psychiatric Association. Name any mental health disorder of the world, you will find them in it. This latest version of the book incorporated suicidal behaviour as one of the disorders requiring psychological treatment. So it named it as 'suicidal behaviour disorder.' The proposal of suicidal behaviour suggested there is as followed.

"A. Within the last 24 months, the individual has made a suicide attempt.

Note: a suicide attempt is a self-initiated sequence of behaviours by an individual who, at the time of initiation, expected that the set of actions would lead to his or her own death. The 'time of initiation" is the time when a behaviour took place that involved applying the method.

The above criteria A specifies that suicide attempt

indicates all the activities done by self-motivation of the victim to end his life. That means he purposes the activities to lead to death. Time of Initiation, according to DSM-V means the time at which he started performing the lethal or life-ending activity.

B. The act does not meet criteria for non-suicidal self-injury….." (American Psychiatric Association. 2013p.g 801)

Criteria B, which states of Non-suicidal self-injury. It specifies that you can diagnose an individual as seriously considered suicide attempt when he does not meet the criteria for Non-suicidal Self-Injury (NSSI), which is as followed.

DSM-5 describes in its proposed criteria for the non-suicidal injury that :

"A. Within the last year, the individual has, on 5 or more days, engaged in intentional self-inflicted damage to the surface of his or her body of a sort likely to induce bleeding, bruising, or pain (e.g., cutting, burning, stabbing, hitting, excessive rubbing), with the expectation that the injury will lead to only minor or moderate physical harm (i.e., there is no suicidal intent).. (p.g., 803)

The above criteria of NSSI state that to diagnose an individual as NSSI, you must have observed that his symptoms are not life-endangering. His behaviour shows that the cutting, bleeding, bruising etc are not so serious. It could also be understood that the individual at the time of injuring himself, has a fear that if he cuts too deep, it may endanger his life. It might be initiated only to gather the attention of those who are close to him.

Moreover, DSM-5 states the diagnostic feature of Non-suicidal self-injury as -

The essential feature of non-suicidal self-injury is that the individual repeatedly inflicts shallow, yet painful injuries to the surface of his or her body. Most commonly, the purpose is to reduce negative emotions, such as tension, anxiety, and self-repraoch, and/or to resolve an interpersonal difficulty. In some cases, the injury is conceived of as a deserved self-punishment. The individual will often report an immediate sensation of relief that occurs during the process. "(P.g., 804)

The above paragraph clearly states the emotional pain, to relieve which the individual engages in NSSI

The above criteria suggested by the DSM-5 is stated here only to know the basic tendencies of suicidal persons, who attempt it with actual intent to die (suicidal behaviour disorder) and those who attempt suicide without injuring their internal muscle tissues or no fatal damage but done only to relieve their emotional pain. But it is strongly recommended to meet psychiatrists if anyone of you or your beloved has the above-described tendencies. Psychiatrists are the only professionals who can suggest medication for severe mental health problems. Clinical Psychologists are the professionals, who will assess your mental health problems and also provide psychotherapies that are best suited for an individual by performing a complete analysis of their personality and mental health profile. So do not use self-help methods or books when it comes to suicidal thoughts or behaviour.

With the above lengthy descriptions of suicidal behaviour disorder and non-suicidal self-injury and suicidal terms, I hope that we all now know what suicide is. This frames the base needed for the journey through suicide valley.

Chapter 2

The Lone Traveler

Imagine that you are travelling on a high-way, and to both sides of your view, you can see the scene where the grass of the crops swaying to the breeze in the atmosphere. Your journey will be relaxing provided you focused on the beauty of the scenery. Then it is a joyful journey because of your focus. You cannot focus on the greenery due to some circumstances like the type of the road (narrow or with bumps) and behaviour of the by-passers. Since your eyes are more attentive to those, you cannot be aware of the peaceful scenery that is constantly being registered into your brain through your eyes. In addition to that if your mind is filled with the stress of your goal (for example, the purpose of your journey like - had to rush to the office for the meeting time is at hand), then you will be missing the serenity offered by nature amidst your journey. In metropolitan cities, where to reach short distances (3 km) too gets an hour, like Mumbai, Hyderabad, Bangalore etc, can we imagine to perceive the beauty (though there are no green fields, small events like children laughing on the roads will be overlooked)? No, we cannot observe these changes in our environment. Hence these days, too many campaigns on Mindfulness are launched all over the World in corporate and educational settings.

The inability to perceive basic natural elements in our environment that could produce inner peace like -a breeze, scenery through the window, children playing etc which are freely available, especially so close to us, had a huge impact on how we perceive our lives as worth living. For a student, his life's worth is exams and peer acceptance. For a homemaker (house-wife) her life's worth is taking care of her children, husband, in-laws, and then comes her own needs. If the needs change like today, women give priority to working in an office for economic sustenance. But also at the same time, she pays attention to taking care of household activities. It gives her no time to do both with her utmost mental capability. Ask her to recollect when she does feel serene last time. She would probably say (if she is a working woman), - "I feel serene when I get time to sleep without any disturbance." She may even remember her pre-marital days when she enjoyed freedom at her father's house.

For an unmarried male, getting a job that could uplift his social status, to get a suitable life partner make life worth living. For a married male, to hold fast to his current employment so that he can take care of his parents, children and wife are top priorities of his life. His life seems to be flourishing when he gets a promotion in job and also when he sees his children growing up happily in his care. So in all these scenarios, each individual's journey of life has different visual fields, where one feels either flourishing ('to grow and develop successfully, ' taken from dictionary.cambrigd.org) or languishing ('lose his vitality, failure,' taken from en.Oxofrddictionaries.com). So those who flourish feel like walking on a pleasant field, if you inquire ever, will note it. But those who are languishing feel doomed to despair. So here in this book, our journey is along with languished individual from a psychological perspective.

Why did the traveller choose this path?

In the introduction of this chapter, we learned that the perspective of the traveller, with which he started his journey determines how he perceives the path - whether serene or gloomy. In turn, it has a significant role in his way of life - flourished or languished. Then the question arises here is -why did he develop such a perspective?

When trying to understand an individual or traveller here, we need to focus on his or her internal environment. This involves how he perceives the external environment with the help of already existing (in-built) patterns of emotions, attitudes and also learned patterns of behaviour. These are components of his personality.

Psychology tries to understand an individual's mental state by examining the individual from both hereditary and environmental factors, which could have a profound influence on the way he behaves so naturally and effortlessly in the social settings. There has been debate over the importance of the "nature-nurture" concept in determining human personality. In an article on this issue, Turkheimer (2018) explained this as followed.

"genes and environment are both crucial to every trait; without genes, the environment would have nothing to work on, and too, genes cannot develop in a vacuum. Even more important, because nature-nurture questions look at the differences among people, the cause of a given trait depends not only on the trait itself but also on the differences in that trait between members of the group being studied. (Turkheimer, E., 2018)"

The above paragraph indicates that genes (nature) and environment (nurture) are both inseparable when explaining the traits that constitute an individual's personality. The development of a trait depends on the group in which he lives.

Genes, heredity and suicidality

The affect of genes on behaviour, especially personality, is observed among clinical patients case records. This is studied as the role of heredity in mental illness. Many times the concept of genes and heredity get confused, overlapped or used as synonymous to each other. But they have conceptual links. Genes (DNA) are transmitted to the next generation and when we explain the behaviour of an individual from the perspective of his genealogy, we use the term heredity. In mental health practice, doctors take the family history of the patients to know whether heredity has an influence on the development of the disorder in the patient. The doctors try to trace out whether the patient's mother, father or one of the grandparents had suffered the same disorder. This will help the doctors in addressing the disorder with proper diagnosis and treatment options.

Now scientists are rigorously working to find out the genes that make one individual vulnerable to commit suicide via heredity. In a meta-analysis carried out to find out which genes are mostly found in suicide attempters, Zai, Clement & Manchia, Mirko et al (2011), have identified that among Psychiatric patients, a gene named Brain-Derived Neurotrophic Factor (BDNF) is related to suicidal behaviour. In specific a low-functioning methionine ("met") variation is found to be a risk factor for suicide among these psychiatric patients (Centre for Addiction and Mental Health, 2011).

Elizabeth Landau (2009) in CNN edition had written an interesting article on suicides where she expressed that '

First-degree relatives are 4 to 6 times more likely to attempt or complete a suicide'

This means that if a person's parents or those who are just one generation ahead of them in their bloodline have suicidal tendencies the susceptibility increases 4 to 6 times. It is an alarming right.

In their book on The neurobiological Basis of Suicide, Zai, de Luca, Strauss, et al. (2012) reviewed previous studies and pointed out that the following evidence provides a link of heredity to suicidality. Especially 48 % is accredited to heredity.

1.   History of Mood Disorders in the family. It means that the individual's family members have either suffered from depression or mania or both

2.   History of family members having bipolar disorder (both depression and mania - individual's state of mood shifts between these two) who have attempted suicide or completed suicide.

3.   Individuals who had depressed mothers who either attempted or completed suicide have more than 50 per cent of the chance to commit suicide in their lifetime.

4.   Twin studies indicated that Mono Zigotic individuals share suicidality. Review showed that

**Table 2: Heritability percentage of suicidality
as per the review of several studies provided by
Zai, de Luca, Strauss, et al. (2012) book**

Type	Gender (unspecified)	Male (with pathology Vietnam Era)	Female	Adolescents
Suicide Ideation	43 %	36%	-	23 %
Suicide plan or attempt	44%	17%	25% (aggression and depression)	38 %
Severe Suicide Attempt	55%			

Recently I watched a Malayalam movie named trance, which is a psychological drama. In that, the protagonist's brother commits suicide. It is that he is suffering from a psychiatric disorder. He refuses to take medication for it. He does beat his brother when he loses his temper. In that movie, while their past is shown, we will come to know that when the protagonist and his brother were still school-going children, one bad day when they returned from school found that there is a crowd around their house who are making commotion while bringing down the dead body of their mother from the ceiling fan to which she hung herself. In the movie, his brother too chose the same way of committing suicide. Like his mother, this one too was successful in completing the suicide.

After watching this my belief got stronger that suicidal behaviour gets imprinted in the minds of the victim's dependents and when they are in a bind to decide a crisis, they chose this path which seems to be the only option left. To suffer from any type of mood disorder or psychiatric disorder is like adding fuel to the burning wood. In case of the above movie scenario too, the victim committed suicide with both modelling and psychiatric disorder reinforcing him to do that.

So in the valley of suicide, the suicidal individual has something happened in his life whether it is from genes or environmental influence, chooses the suicide attempt as the last resort.

We have already seen the sociological perspective of defining forms of suicide. Now let us look at the psychological parameters. Many Psychologists tried to take a peek into the minds of suicide attempted persons, who fortunately survived it. Some are derived from interviewing the victims' relatives and case reports of the doctors who treated the victims.

This can be studied under two headings.

1.   Perceptions of the suicidal person-how he receives external environment

2.   Personality variables-how he reacts to the external environment as per one's biological, characteristic predispositions.

1. Perceptions of the Suicidal person

The traveller's (suicidal person) psychological status can be explained from -cognitive (higher mental functioning like thinking, problem-solving, reasoning etc), affective (feeling, emotion) and motor activity (i.e., real action shown in the form of writing or all human performance done through the moving of one's body parts to end oneself-like cutting one's body, taking poison etc.) factors.

Edwin Shneidman , father of suicidology described 10 commonalities which explain the

'psychological threads of suicide.'

I am herewith adding "conveys" column to debrief them by comparing it with the article by Antoon A. Leenaars (2010) and Suicidepreventioncommunity.files.wordpress.com. (2018)

Table 3 Dr Edwin Shneidman's 10 Commonalities

No.	Commonality	Conveys
i.	The common **purpose** of suicide is to **seek a solution.**	To end internal suffering due to the problem situation
ii.	The common **goal** of suicide is the **cessation of consciousness** consciousness as the	The suicidal individual interprets the end of only way to end the suffering."
III.	The common **stimulus** in suicide is **intolerable psychological pain.**	Psychache- "intolerable emotion, unbearable pain, unacceptable anguish."
IV.	The common **stressor** in suicide is **frustrated with psychological needs.**	"psychological needs that are not being met" will be the stressor
V.	The common **emotion** in suicide is **hopelessness-helplessness.**	"feels despondent, utterly unsalvageable"
VI.	The common **cognitive state** in suicide is **ambivalence.**	"wish to die and they simultaneously wish to be rescued."
VII.	The common **perceptual state** in suicide is **constriction.**	Could only see "two choices -either continue suffering or die."
VIII.	The common **action** in suicide is **egression**-(a way out, such as a path; exit)*	Does all actions like leaving the job as it gives stress; running away from home etc.
IX.	The common **interpersonal** act in suicide is the **communication of intention.**	Gives clues of his helpless state to the family and and significant other.
X.	The common consistency in suicide is with lifelong coping patterns.	"A person's past tendency for black-and-white thinking escapism, control, capitulation and the like could serve as a clue to how he or she might deal with a present crisis."

Egress definition and meaning.[Def.2] Collins English Dictionary. (n.d.). Retrieved from https://www.collinsdictionary.com/dictionary/english/egress

Researches following the footsteps of Shneidman, conducted several studies and found the suicidal tendencies as followed.

Caroline Maskill and Dr Ian Hodges, Velma McClellan, Dr Sunny Collings (2005) in a report for Ministry of Health, New Zeland discussed the social-psychological model of the suicide of Taylor (1982) as followed.

"In this model, there are two outcomes: suicide acts that are either an 'ordeal'. or are 'purposive'. These outcomes depend on the degree of certainty or uncertainty that the suicidal person feels, and also their degree of attachment or detachment from other people (presumably some indication of their social integration)."

Here, ordeal refers to suicide as a consequence of unpleasant life experiences of an individual which he or she withhold with a lot of energy. Purposive indicates an intentional act of an individual to commit suicide. These researchers also explained that it depends on the tendency of an individual, his attraction, especially dependency or dejection of attachment need. It shows two extremes, too much attachment to people or too much detachment from people.

In the following figure, we are going to understand the conflict of a suicidal individual. He is unable to resolve as he had to consider a whole lot like - certainty, uncertainty, attachment and detachment values that are presented to him by his life circumstances.

Figure 2 Taylor's Social Psychological Model of Suicide

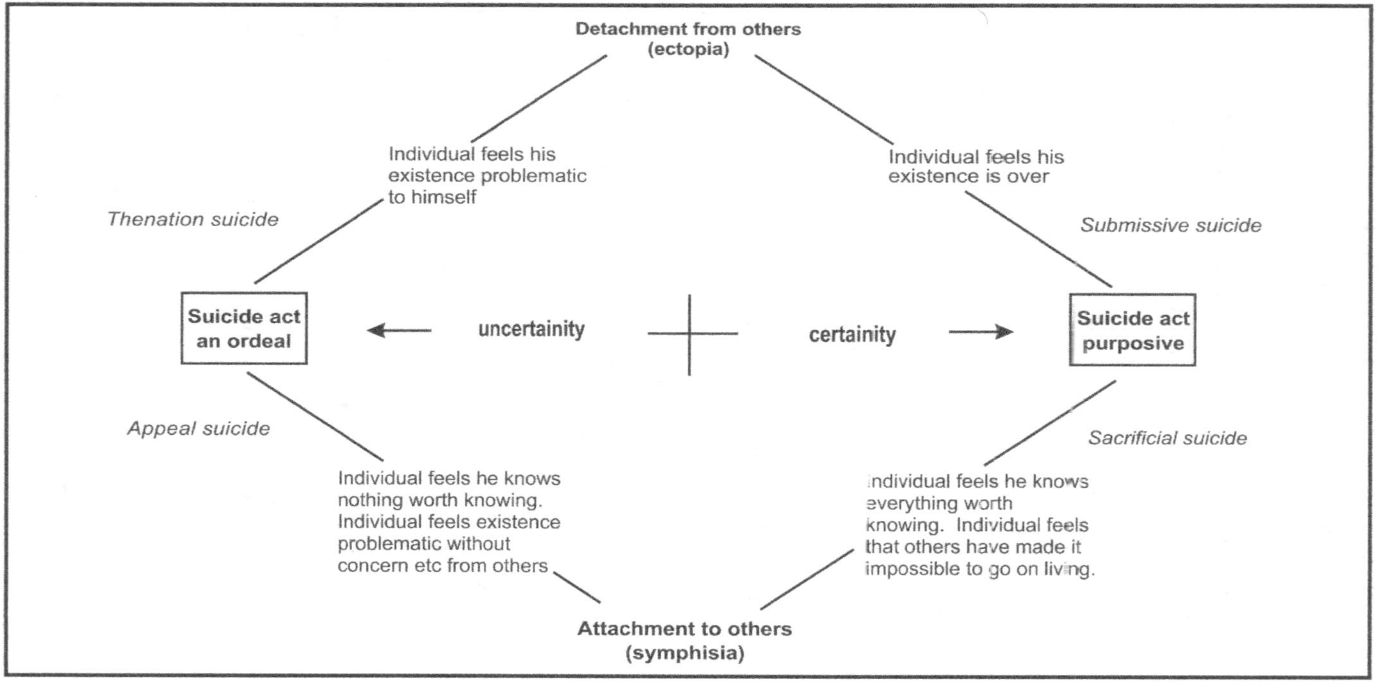

Credit: Caroline Maskill and Dr Ian Hodges, Velma McClellan, Dr Sunny Collings (2005) The above figure has been taken out from **https://www.health.govt.nz/system/files/documents/ publications/explainingpatternsofsuicide.pdf**

In the above figure, the researchers explained the process clearly but I suggest the readers look top to down in the way the arrows are leaning towards. There the conflict that the individual is going through is explained beautifully.

2. Personality Variables

As Eysenck (1971) defined, personality is

"the more or less stable and enduring organization of a person's character, temperament, intellect and physique, which determine his unique adjustment to the environment" (cited by Mangal, 2002)

In simple terms,

"an individual's unique and relatively stable patterns of behaviour, thoughts and emotions or the psychological forces that make people uniquely themselves." (Robert Baron, 2001)

Jess Fiest and Gregory Fiest (2006) defined personality as -

"a pattern of relatively permanent traits and unique characteristics that give both consistency and individuality to a person's behaviour. Traits contribute to individual differences in behaviour, consistency of behaviour over time and stability of behaviour across situations. Traits may be unique, common to some group or shared by the entire species, but their pattern is different for each individual. Characteristics are unique qualities of an individual that include such attributes as temperament, physique and intelligence."

So, personality in the public mindset refers mainly to the "traits' exhibited by the individuals that are observable in the social interactions. These are verified by the observers in different situations and if the same trait is observed in different situations, the individual's personality is explained by that trait.

"typical examples being shyness, honesty, tidiness and stupidity" (Andrew Colman, 2006)

J. Mark C. Williams, Leslie R. Pollock (2000) have compiled an article on the psychology of suicidal behaviour, in which these researchers pointed out that the personality variables that are observed in suicide attempters are neuroticism (in repcated attempts), impulsivity, perfectionism, the tendency to withdraw and aloofness.

Let us carefully examine thc above traits.

Neuroticism

According to the Cambridge Dictionary of Psychology, Neuroticism is defined as

-" n. 1. The degree to which an individual chronically engages in dysfunctional emotional, behavioral, and cognitive actions. 2. One of the putative "big five" dimensions of personality, which measures the frequency of experiencing negative emotions, tendency to interpret stimuli as threatening, social withdrawal, and a tendency to react with stress to minor frustrations at the high end and emotional stability and positive emotions at the low end. (David Matsumoto, 2009 p.g., 336)

Big five dimensions of personality is a measure to assess the basic personality traits of individuals. The above definition showed that neurotic are too emotional and their interpretation is too extreme. But neuroticism was beautifully explained in Britannica.com, an online dictionary, which is as followed:

"Neuroticism, in psychology and development, a broad personality trait dimension representing the degree to which a person experiences the world as distressing, threatening, and

unsafe. Each individual can be positioned somewhere on this personality dimension between extreme poles: perfect emotional stability versus complete emotional chaos. Highly neurotic individuals tend to be labile (that is, subject to frequently changing emotions), anxious, tense, and withdrawn. Individuals who are low in neuroticism tend to be content, confident, and stable. The latter report fewer physical and psychological problems and less stress than do highly neurotic individuals. (Kwon & Weed, 2006)

Many studies emphasized that elevated neurotic symptoms were found in individuals who reported suicide ideation (Rappaport, Flint, Kendler, 2017). Especially higher levels of neuroticism are the most predominant trait of psychiatric patients who attempted suicide (Bo Bi*, Wei Liu, Die Zhou, Xu Fu, Xiaoxia Qin and Jiali Wu, 2017). But often people suffering from neuroticism do not recognize the symptoms as unnatural and do not meet the psychiatrists. Research shows that such people were suffering from interpersonal problems such as

'pathologic family structure in communication, roles, affective involvement and general family function' (Sahraian, Ebrahimi, Toubaei, Ahmadzadeh, Mani, 2016).

Neuroticism predicted that perceived burdensomeness thwarted belongingness process involved in interpersonal relationships as leading to suicide ideation among young adults (Marc Baertschi, Alessandra Costanza, Alessandra Canuto and Kerstin Weber, 2018). It is understandable that when one feels that he or she is a burden to the family or unwanted could develop neuroticism.

Individuals who have both neuroticism and anxiety attachment are 3.99 times higher risk of repeat suicide attempt (Pennel L, Quesada JL, Dematteis M, 2018). Neuroticism predicts suicide ideation in both men and women alike. For women, it predicts depression whereas for men it does not (Peters, John, Bowen, Baetz, & Balbuena, 2018).

Neuroticism is treatable. In a study, it was shown that certain symptoms of neuroticism which are unique to men and women with suicide ideation, were reduced through psychotherapy. The psychotherapy focused on the interpersonal problems using psychodynamic approaches. These approaches focus on defence mechanisms that a neurotic uses as a way to be resistant to the treatment procedure. These researchers explained that

> *"Important elements of treatment were: work with resistance and transference, strengthening ego and autonomy of patients, correcting dysfunctional cognitive schemas and to enable patients to experience corrective relationships and experiences."*

These quoted elements address the thinking pattern of the patients which hinder the therapeutic process thereby no adaptive change will take place in the patient's condition. Cognitive restructuring is carried out for such patients using psychodynamic therapies. It addresses negative thinking patterns that are developed due to interpersonal conflicts at the prominent developmental stages of life such as infancy, childhood and adolescence.

In addition to the above, they have observed that the neurotic personality traits that were reduced as a result of the psychodynamic approaches also seem to differ in both genders. For male, these were -

> *"Negative self-esteem, Impulsiveness, Sense of alienation, Demobilization, Difficulties in emotional relations, Lack of vitality, Sense of lack of control, Sense of guilt, Difficulties in interpersonal*

relations, Sense of being in danger, Exaltation, Ponderings."

These quoted traits observed in males project the need that these male express. Their needs are more ego defensive. It means they struggle to hold on their emotions and to act in accordance to others wishes. For instance, defensiveness is visible in Negative self-esteem, Impulsiveness, Sense of alienation, Demobilization. The remaining indicate his need to showcase himself in a presentable form in his dealings with others (interpersonal interactions).

For female, the traits are -

"Feeling of being dependent on the Environment, Asthenia (abnormal weakness or lack of energy), Difficulties with decision making, Conviction of own resourcelessness in life, Deficit in internal locus of control and Imagination indulging in fiction." (Rodzi?ski, Rutkowski, Soba?ski, Mielim?ka, etal.,2015).

For female, these traits indicate a lack of independence in living. For them, they are compelled to live according to the instructions of the family members. They are brought up in a way that they incline involuntarily to be submissive to their parents, husbands and even to children. These could be the actual culprits of neuroticism in females.

Impulsivity

In Cambridge Dictionary of Psychology, impulsivity is defined as - *A characteristic or trait in which the individual tends to act quickly on motives as they arise with little reflection as to the consequences of his or her actions or their effect on others or on plans for satisfying other motives.* (David Matsumoto, 2009 p.g., 252)

Impulsivity in a simple sense could be imagined as any action which an individual does without thinking. An impulsive individual just acts upon a spur of the moment. You just get a spark of thought urging you to scribble something and do so without hesitation, this exemplifies impulsiveness. This impulsiveness is different from insight. Insight comes after you tried hard to solve something for a long time and when you are about to give up, a thought, which was the output of your brain processors, comes at the unexpected time like a spark. Whereas impulsiveness is just a sensation which is fleeting and lasts only for a few seconds, but you act immediately upon the thought which came up like a spark. Both are sparks but insight is the outcome of deliberate thinking processes and so is productive. But impulsive behaviour is on the spot spark which doesn't have a profound basis and is destructive. So those who are impulsive often perform self-harm actions such as suicide attempts.

Impulsiveness is a predictive trait for those individuals who exhibit suicidal behaviour even among those without any psychiatric disorders, in addition to aggression (Bo Bi*, Wei Liu, Die Zhou, Xu Fu, Xiaoxia Qin and Jiali Wu, 2017). This study was done in China and similar findings were found in a study done on Idu Mishmi tribe of Arunachal Pradesh, India. Here the researchers found that the population of Idu Mishmi tribe scored high on impulsivity trait with a mean of 73.56, which was greater than the records available for rural(61.71) and urban(62.65) impulsivity scores in the region. Though the female scored high (74.5) on impulsivity than the male in the tribe, exhibited auto-aggression, a form of aggression in which the aggression felt is inverted into oneself. Though men scored less (72.73) than women in impulsivity score, more men attempted suicide. The researchers explained that men in this tribe used physical aggression or violence in action like the destruction of property. In particular, the results could be seen in the perspective that *the traits of impulsivity and aggression are deeply correlated among males'* (Singh, Rao, 2018). This shows that impulsivity differs from male to female in terms of action related to suicide. One research finding pointed out that those who have conduct problems had a higher risk of attempting suicide whereas those who have identity problems and gender moderated impulsivity do have suicide ideation (Jelena Brezo, Joel Paris, Richard Tremblay, Frank Vitaro, 2006). In simple terms, those who have behavioural problems (external disorders) attempt suicide while those with internalized problems (keep everything in one's internal state) such as identity crisis, impulsivity (which is gender varied), have suicide ideation. That means these only think about suicide do not attempt it. This could be the reason why Idu Mishmi tribe women did not commit suicide but might have suicide ideation. Whereas it could be clearly and confidently said about men of Idu Mishmi tribe that their conduct problems dominated their impulsivity and was observed in high rates of suicide attempts in Idu Mishmi men. The point I would like you all to focus here is that -impulsivity is a predictor of suicide ideation and suicide attempts' but one should look at the gender also. Impulsive suicide attempters do not plan. They just carryout the vague suicide thought that pops in their mind at the moment. Moreover, these impulsive suicide attempters were younger (21.89 average age) than the non-impulsive suicide attempters (28.61 years average age) (Meerae Lim, Soojung Lee and Jong-Ik Park, 2016).

Perfectionism

We all have seen movie actors, theatre artists and creative individuals often not getting satisfied with their work performance. They even go to the extremity of not eating, sleeping or sitting night out to make their work pleasant to their mind or they compare it with a measuring rod (yardstick) which they set-up themselves. They also think constantly about those whom it is targeted. Will it please my fans? But often they find faults with their acting or performance. It might have been fantastic to the fans. But it is not so to the actor. This is an epitome of the trait 'Perfectionism.'

American Psychological Association's (APA) Dictionary of Psychology defined perfectionism as

> - *"n. the tendency to demand of others or of oneself an extremely high or even flawless level of performance, in excess of what is required by the situation. It is associated with depression, anxiety, eating disorders, and other mental health problems. -perfectionist adj., n. (Gary VandenBos, 2015, pg 778)"*

According to the Cambridge Dictionary of Psychology, Perfectionism is defined as-

> *"n. Perfectionism refers to a trait-based tendency to hold extremely high expectations of the self or others and to expect such performance from self or others in goal pursuit. (David Matsumoto, 2009 p.g., 369)"*

In the above two variations of definitions, we can observe that APA emphasized perfectionism to the flawlessness of performance that is going above the limit or requirement of the task. This tendency of individuals leads to some forms of mental health disorders which are the consequence of maintaining this perfectionism. On the other hand, the Cambridge Dictionary version reflected the internal tendency of the perfectionist about his performance.

Research shows that perfectionism is linked to suicide ideation and suicide attempts. This link was first published by Psychologist Sidney Blatt in his influential work entitled "The Destructiveness of Perfectionism Implications for the treatment of depression" for in American Psychologist Journal of American Psychological Association in 1995. Jarett C, the editor of British Psychological Society Reader's Digest, quoted Blatt's statements as followed-

> *"Because of the need to maintain a personal and public image of strength and perfection, [perfectionists] are constantly trying to prove themselves, are always on trial, feel vulnerable to any possible implication of failure or criticism, and often are unable to turn to others, even the closest of confidants, for help or to share their anguish," Blatt wrote. (Jarrett, 2017, July 27).*

Perfectionism should not be considered in a negative context, but some researchers made a distinction between two types of perfectionism. Especially, Hamachek in 1980, distinguished between two forms namely *'adaptive and maladaptive perfectionism'*. He says adaptive perfectionism involves a task completion where the performer has adequate awareness of his strengths and weaknesses, task nature, circumstances that could affect the task completion and have realistic expectations of goals. The task well-done is the reward for him which gives genuine self-satisfaction.

'High levels of functioning are pursued to the maximum of one's ability while maintaining internal and external balance and in life.'

An Adaptive perfectionist does not include over-estimation of one's capability to complete the task with greater expectations. Thus not succeeding in the task would not make the adaptive perfectionist crumble to guilt or self-defeat. Hamcheck named this adaptive perfectionism as 'normal perfectionism' (Lessin, Pardo,2017). While performing a task, an adaptive perfectionist takes into account his or her strengths and weakness and do not put unrealistic goals, which are not possible to attain. In a simple sense,

'normal or adaptive perfectionists strive for high standards resulting in feelings of accomplishment and satisfaction. (Santhi Periasamy and Jeffrey Ashby, 2002)'

For example, let us consider that a young man is preparing for an exam for which there is a prescribed syllabus. If the young man is an adaptive perfectionist, he would first visualize his learning style, goal (i.e., the portion to be covered and the time limit etc) to complete the preparation. He will not be rigid in completing the task in stipulated time by rushing to read it on the go. He knows well how to adjust the timing according to his physical strength, tiredness and sometimes unavoidable tasks like helping parents, siblings etc in their works. Ultimately he will finish his preparation and he would not be intimidated by the expectation of getting high marks or failure. But he fixes his goal high. His perfectionism enables him to work hard until he can be sure that his performance is perfect or his goal is achieved. It is a task-oriented perfectionism. I think adaptive perfectionism lacks these days in the majority of the students of all age groups.

Hamacheck made another distinction of perfectionism i.e, *'maladaptive perfectionism'*. He referred it with the name *'neurotic perfectionism'*. To make it simple, it is the manifestation of neurotic behaviour observed in the in-between processes starting from task origination to completion processes.

"Neurotic or maladaptive perfectionists strive for high standards but, no matter the result, "never seem to do things good enough."

Hamacheck further explains that -while adaptive perfectionists put high standards and attain the successful result that is satisfactory, maladaptive put high standards but do not have their mental scale of the goodness of fit that would be a benchmark to compare and get satisfied with it. In simple terms, they do not agree with the judgment of goodness of their work as they couldn't explain what the good in their view represents is (Santhi Periasamy and Jeffrey Ashby, 2002).

It is observed that the maladaptive perfectionist never gets satisfied even if the work is praised by others as he had high internal expectations (self-frame of reference) about how the task should look like when it is completed. So his life revolves around doing every task he gets to do, with perfection, ie., precision. A flawless performance is his goal. Hence these two types are considered as Evaluative Concerns Perfectionism (ECP-adaptive perfectionism) and Personal Standards Perfectionism (PSP-maladaptive perfectionism) in research review articles (Lessin, Pardo, 2017).

Majority of research articles on Perfectionism are done on 'maladaptive perfectionism' and its link to mental health concerns such as stress, anxiety depression and suicidal behaviour. In particular, research shows that the risk of death is more among perfectionists and neurotics (Fry, Debats, 2009). This Maladaptive perfectionism found to be developing depression among adolescents by the age of 15 years. This is observed through paternal (father) psychological control over the children (Socnens, Bart & Luyckx, Koen & Vansteenkiste, Maarten & Luyten, Patrick & Duriez, Bart & Goossens, Luc., 2008).

When both parents had disputes between themselves, observing late adolescents' try to internalize the high standards that these parents put for them. This is found to develop over-sensitivity and is manifested in the late adolescents' in form of doubts over their actions and thereby these put high personal standards. These seem to lead to perfectionism in them. For these adolescents, lack of emotional support and to rely on decisions of their parents have been observed. (Gong, Xiaopeng & Paulson, Sharon & Wang, Cen, 2016)

Paternal psychological control as per research culminates different forms maladaptive perfectionism. So for your understanding here are the main forms of maladaptive perfectionism

Hewitt and Flett in their

"multidimensional perfectionism scales (MPS)" mentioned three types of perfectionism, namely- Other- Oriented, Self-Oriented and Socially Prescribed

Other-Oriented Perfectionism refers to

'the perfectionist's demand that others meet exaggerated and unrealistic standards.'

Here, others represent significant people like parents, siblings etc of the perfectionist (Lessin, Pardo,2017; Pychyl,. , 2008, April 30).

Self-Oriented Perfectionism relates to

"the exceedingly high, self-imposed, unrealistic standards that perfectionists feel they must meet. They are unable to accept flaws or shortcomings in themselves, and engage in intense self-scrutiny when they encounter any sign of personal failure."

Due to the high standards and relentless self-criticism, these perfectionists show increased rates of depression. (Lessin, Pardo, 2017)" This is what we observe in actors who would not accept external praises unless their performance on screen would be satisfying the criteria that they had (mental image of the scene) for 'perfect action' is met in their mind's eye. This type of perfectionism develops when children absorb their fathers' directed expectations for them while striving for their father's praise for their efforts to please him. So as days go by, this need of getting father's praise of their efforts (mostly academic achievement) becomes a habit and thus results in self-oriented perfectionism among these children (Sabry Abd-El-Fattah, Hessa Abdulrahman Fakhroo, 2012).

Socially Prescribed Perfectionism,

"is maintained by a belief that others hold exaggerated expectations that are nearly impossible to meet, but that must be reached in order to gain approval and acceptance. This type of perfectionism combines intrapersonal achievement stressors with perceived interpersonal pressure (Lessin, Pardo, 2017)."

This form is the major source of suicide potential but not depression and hopelessness among psychiatric patients. The suicidal potential is found among individuals who are overwhelmed by the unrealistic expectations others have for them (Hewitt, Flett, Turnbull-Donovan, 1992). The reason is that socially prescribed perfectionist has- *negative evaluations of social comparison, submissive behaviour, shame and defeat among undergraduate students* (Rachael Wyatt, Paul Gilbert, 1998) ." In children and adolescents who have socially prescribed perfectionism, the attitude of not displaying (expressing) one's imperfection to maintain the social image of himself as perfect and covering up one's problems like being bullied, predict future suicide attempts. Social hopelessness experienced by these is the main reason. (Roxborough, Hewitt, Kaldas, Flett, Caelian, Sherry, Sherry, 2012). He is taking in others expectations and he feels hopeless to meet their standards. He is crushed in spirit to please others. In particular, socially prescribed perfectionists long for the approval and recognition of significant others and in the process of doing so develop insecurity feelings such as 'what will happen if I don't meet their high expectations of me? So the inability to cope with these pressures the perfectionists, though have normal health, commit suicide (Kiamanesh, Dyregrov, Haavind, Dieserud, 2014). Socially Prescribed perfectionism can predict suicide potential among depressed adolescents. It increases unbearable pain as these would not be satisfied with life. Coupled with chronic daily stress experienced by these depressed adolescents, it increases suicide potential beyond hopelessness and helplessness (Paul Hewitt, Carmen Caelian Chang Chen and Gordon Flett, 2014). Finally, it should be noted that socially prescribed perfectionism, non-display of imperfection increases suicide ideation. If one exhibits or experiences socially prescribed perfectionism, it is naïve to interpret that he will commit suicide Arezoo Shahnaz, Boaz. Saffer, David Klonsky, 2018). It is described here with the intention that the parents who are reading this would take care that their children, adolescents have not developed this kind of perfectionism. A recent study showed that academic achievement increases perfectionism strivings ('self-oriented perfectionism, personal standards')and concerns (socially prescribed perfectionism, concern over mistakes, doubts about actions, discrepancy, perfectionistic attitudes) (Martin M. Smith et al 2018). If you children and adolescent have academic efficacy(the belief that they can achieve academically up to certain grade), it only develops perfectionistic strivings, means try to be perfect in academic (Damian, Stoeber, Negru?Subtirica, and B?ban, 2017;). Kindly see to it that they would not develop any of the mentioned perfectionistic types. Please pay attention to your children and adolescents who are sensitive to mistakes as the research shows that this is linked to depression, which could if unnoticed and treated could lead to suicide ideation (Lence Milosevaa and Tatjana Vukosavljevic-Gvozden, 2014).

Research in these days also magnifies other personality traits like Emotional Maturity, psychological maturity, self-criticism, harm-avoidance and Self-directedness, which will be discussed below.

Emotional maturity-Psychological Maturity

Emotional Maturity as per Dictionary of American Psychological Association is defined as

"a high and appropriate level of emotional control and expression

(Gary VandenBos, 2015, p.g., 364)"

According to psychology wiki

"Emotional maturity is a personality trait, the result of emotional development and the display of emotion appropriate to ones chronological age. it usually reflects increased emotional adjustment and emotional stability and the attainment of emotional self-regulation" (Emotional maturity, 2018)

Components of emotional maturity: In an article on "Emotional Maturity: Characteristics and Levels", Dr Umesh Chandra Kapri and Dr Neelam Rani (2014), have pointed out Dr Jerome Murray's explanation of these characteristics, which are -

"Easy Flow of Love & Affection, Face To Face With Reality, Hands on Experience of Life, Taking Criticism Positively, Hopefulness, Interested in Giving as in Receiving, Ability to Learn from Experience, The Ability to Handle Hostility Constructively and Open-Minded."

After reading the above definitions, one will understand that emotional maturity leads to living in true happiness as one manages emotions well in his social interactions. With emotional maturity, living is bliss in any circumstance.

Whereas a similar concept called psychological maturity is found to be associated with suicide ideation. Psychological Maturity is defined by APA's Dictionary of Psychology as -

"the ability to deal effectively and resiliently with experience and to perform satisfactorily in developmental tasks (biological, social, cognitive) characteristic of one's age level. (Gary VandenBos, 2015, p.g., 858)"

Here I would like to clarify the slight difference between both types of maturity. Emotional maturity refers to one's ability to deal with emotions appropriate for the chronological age, but psychological maturity, in addition to emotions also considers other tasks -with resilience as the important aspect, which covers all the three aspects of human functioning - biological(internal environment of the body), social (external environment/ interpersonal interactions) and cognition (thinking and other higher-order mental function).

Research shows that there is an indirect link between emotional maturity and suicide ideation among youth. Emotional maturity when coupled with depression could best explain its relationship to suicide ideation. It means that depression affects the emotional maturity of an individual making him think about suicide ideation. In addition to this emotional maturity of the individual, psychological maturity (self-reliance) is also important (Morales-Vives, Fabia & Dueñas, Jorge Manuel, 2018). When emotional self-efficacy (ability to control or keep one's emotions in check) reduced, suicide ideation, suicide attempts increase among Males irrespective of colour -i.e, white or black (Valois, Robert & Zullig, Keith & Hunter, Amy, 2013).

Self-Criticism

American Psychological Association's Dictionary of Psychology defined 'Self-criticism' as

"self-criticism n. the evaluation of one's own behaviour and attributes, with recognition of one's weaknesses, errors, and shortcomings. Although self-criticism can have a positive effect in fostering personal growth, a tendency toward harsh self-

criticism is thought by some to be a risk factor for depression. - self-critical adj. (Gary VandenBos, 2015, p.g., 954)"

The Cambridge Dictionary of Psychology defined it as

"self-criticism -n. The evaluative examination of one's own mental processes and behavior. Overly harsh or negative evaluation of the self is associated with depression (David Matsumoto, 2009 p.g., 467)".

Self-criticism could be imagined as a judgment given by the reality show judges who judge the performance of the artists. Here both the judge and the performer are the same. Here the standards for judging oneself are maintained either by fixing the opinion that others are superior or hostile towards them (comparative self-criticism) or by setting up standards that minimize the success in light of superior goals one has (internalized criticism). In Internalized criticism, the self-critic would accept only absolute success. There should not be any comparison in or outside of himself regarding the task he did. These two types of self-criticism are coined by "Thompson and Zuroff, in 2004, in the process of constructing 'The Levels of Self-Criticism Scale'. This is observed in children concerning academic achievement (Liya Panayotova, Mar 27, 2016). Research shows that people have two kinds of self-talking in which one reassures activities ('Caring emphatic self -cared for, soothed self') done so far and another form is which that hurts, criticizes ('Hostile dominant self - fearful, subordinated self') whatever one does in a day. It is observed that when an individual's thinking style is dominated by frustration, the inner voice would be of anger, especially of 'self-attacking.' When the individual is motivated to improve and correct himself too much, that type of thinking style refers to the 'self-critical' inner voice. But when the thinking style of an individual is overpowered by the thoughts of hurting or destroying oneself, it is referred to be 'hating self (Prof Paul Gilbert, n.d.).' Self- critical individual would not be able to imagine himself as a warm, empathetic and supportive person. So he tends to reflect on negative self-image. So when it comes to criticizing himself, he shows his anger, frustration and power to show himself he is in control of his life (Paul Gilbert, Mark Baldwin, Chris Irons, Jodene Baccus and Michelle Palmer, 2006).

Self-criticism has, as per the measures of self-criticism, three forms which serve two basic functions:

Forms:

1.   **Inadequate self** -criticizing lack of one's abilities, resourcefulness etc.

2.   **Reassured self** - accepting and empathetic about one's good qualities

3.   **Hated Self** - Unacceptable self-image because of self and others' standards

Functions:

1. Self-correction

2. Self-persecution

To put it simply, an individual adapts self-criticism which serves the functions of self-correction and self-preservation and manifested to the observer in the above mentioned three forms. Self-criticism (internalized shame) and external shame seemed to mutually enhance one another and lead to anxiety and depressive symptomatology among people visiting psychiatric clinics in Portuguese(Castilho, Paula & Pinto-Gouveia, José & Duarte, Joana, 2016).

Self-criticism develops in children through maladaptive parental practices. Every child desires the attention of its parents and when this basic need is not met then there is a high probability of resulting in emotional distress which persists even when they become adults (Falgares, Marchetti, Manna, Musso, Oasi, Kopala-Sibley, De Santis and Verrocchio, 2018). When parents reject their children, the memory along with the emotion that the children experience at that moment, never be forgotten as these get 'anchored' (deep-rooted) in their minds. When children perceive lack of Parental care, it would generate shame feelings which in turn develops in them depression (Sandquist, Grenyer & Caputi, 2009). The words that the parents use to criticize their children become a reference with which these children criticize themselves when faced with negative outcomes in their life. For example, if an uncaring parent criticizes the child saying "you are worthless, the child in other difficult situation, uses the same word by replacing "you" by "I". That is, the child directs his self-image by criticizing it "I am worthless" and then keeps on repeating the same and in long run, this leads to depression. When children perceive no parental care (insecure anxiety and the avoidant attachment style of parents) they gradually develop self-criticism (hated self), depression, which in long run increases suicidal risk, especially Non-suicidal Self Injury (NSSI) (Falgares, Marchetti, Manna, Musso, Oasi, Kopala-Sibley, De Santis and Verrocchio, 2018; Baetens, Imke & Claes, Laurence & Hasking, Penelope & Smits, Dirk & Grietens, Hans & Onghena, Patrick & Martin, Graham. 2013; Gilbert, Paul & Clarke, M & Hempel, Susanne & Miles, Jeremy

& Irons, Chris, 2004). It is that recollection of parental rejections increase self-criticism and so increases depressive symptoms which lead to suicide behaviour (Campos, Rui & Besser, Avi & Blatt, Sidney, 2013). One of the crucial symptoms of depression that is leading to suicide is 'brooding rumination.' Treynor et al (2003) defined Brooding rumination as -

"a passive comparison of one's current situation with some unachieved standard" (cited by Brandon Gibb, Marie Grassia, Lindsey Stone, and Dorothy . Uhrlass and John McGeary , 2012).

Self-critical Individuals with brooding rumination showed suicide ideation (O'Connor, Rory & Noyce, Rosie, 2008). The standards (past/present) that self-critical adolescents maintain were compared with the on-going problems like peer hassles (e.g. Bullying, social comparison) and the accumulated depression lead to NSSI (Xavier, Ana & Pinto-Gouveia, José & Cunha, Marina, 2016). Childhood maltreatment of parents, especially emotional abuse, sexual abuse contributed to self-criticism and in turn strong NSSI behaviour among adolescents (Glassman, Lisa & Weierich, Mariann & Hooley, Jill & Deliberto, Tara & Nock, Matthe, 2007). Number of times the individual tries to attempt NSSI is found to be resulting from the parental criticism, lack of parental emotional support, which made the individual develop self-criticism and thereby depression (Baetens, Imke & Claes, Laurence & Hasking, Penelope & Smits, Dirk & Grietens, Hans & Onghena, Patrick & Martin, Graham, 2013)

Research shows that self-critical individuals perceive the external criticisms too personal and to escape psychic struggle thus arise, attempt suicide and this phenomenon is observed even among normal individuals (Campos, Rui & Holden,

Ronald & Baleizão, Cristina & Caçador, Berta & Sofia Fragata, Ana, 2018; Fazaa, Norman & Page, Stewart, 2003). Being self-critical, the individual would not seek others help when needed. The psychological distress experienced by self-critical individuals becomes a trigger to suicide attempts (Rui Campos, Ronald Holden, Cristina Baleizão, Berta Caçador & Ana Sofia Fragata , 2018). Research shows that in comparison to hated self, another form of self-criticism, i.e., the inadequate self is the major cause of suicide behaviour. The reason is that-"self-criticism triggers threat and defensive emotions and behaviours, which lead to negative emotions that are difficult to regulate; thus, different kinds of psychopathology, like suicide behaviours, occur. (Hamid Khanipour, Mitra Hakim shooshtari and Reza Bidaki 2016)."

One way to resolve the negative effect of self-criticism turning into depressive symptoms is to inculcate the habit of self-compassion. This is found to decrease depressive symptoms in African Americans of low income. This is found to be effective irrespective of ethnicity according to positive psychology research (Zhang, Huaiyu & Watson-Singleton, Natalie & Pollard, Sara & Pittman Delishia & Lamis, Dorian & Fischer, Nicole & Patterson, Bobbi & Kaslow, Nadine, 2017)

Harm Avoidance

According to the American Psychological Association Dictionary of Psychology –

Harm avoidance is the *"sensitivity to, and avoidance of, punishing stimuli. (Gary VandenBos, 2015, p.g.,195)"*

It is very instinctual even for a toddler to avoid a candle which is with fire because he knows that it is dangerous to his body. In more colloquial terms, when a woman uses a knife to chop vegetables, she pays a lot of attention to avoid her fingers being cut in the process. It does indicate that we humans have a tendency to avoid harmful substances and an event alike. But when it comes to suicide behaviour, harm-avoidance has as a personality trait has much to offer when thinking about who attempts suicide. High Harm avoidance is found to develop depression among normal individuals. In specific it determines when it starts (onset) and how it develops into Major Depressive Disorder (Saigo, Hayashida, Tayama, Ogawa, Bernick, Takeoka, Shirabe, 2018). It develops in a child through interpersonal sensitivity issues such as parental (both mother and father) care and affection. When parents follow authoritarian controlling and over protectiveness, there is a greater probability that the harm avoidance nature that these children get habituated to results in suicide attempts (Gau, Susan & Chen, Ying-Yeh & Tsai, Fang-Ju & Lee, Ming-Been & Chiu, Yen-Nan & Soong, Wei-Tsuen & Hwu, Hai-Gwo. , 2010). Let us imagine how over-protectiveness creates harm avoidance in children. In overprotective families, parents do every task and the child has to just follow what the parent instructs him to do in whatever place he goes to. For example, to school, shopping malls etc, these parents do every task and the children will be just observers. This prolonged care of the parents even after teenage would make the child dependent on parents rather than on his self. In such situations, if the teen faces any adversity such as ragging at college junior welcoming party, would lead to a suicide attempt. Let us now examine the actual components of harm avoidance that lead to suicide attempts as per scientific research.

Harm avoidance is the peculiar personality trait that is found to be associated strongly with suicide behaviour, in specific suicide attempts. The suicide attempted individuals tend to experience Anticipatory Worry and Pessimism, Fear of Uncertainty, Shyness with Strangers and Fatigability (Raffaella Calati, Ina Giegling, Dan Rujescu, Annette Hartmann, Hans-Jurgen Moller, Diana De Ronchi, Alessandro Serretti, 2008). It is that harm avoidance creates hopelessness among suicide individuals. Especially fear of uncertainty is the temperamental trait associated with harm avoidance among women who attempted suicide. The components of Harm avoidance that are mentioned above produce depressive symptoms and thereby have a higher probability of suicide thoughts (Mehmet Yumru, Haluk Savas, Hasan Herken, Hanifi Kokacya, 2009; Liu, Shen-Ing & Huang, Yu-Hsin & Wu, Ying-Hui & Huang, Kuo-Yang & Huang, Hui-Chun & Sun, Fang-Ju & Huang, Chiu-Ron & Sung, Ming-Ru & Huang, Yo-Ping., 2017). Hence it is advised to screen for harm avoidance among college students as screening for depression and harm avoidance and carrying out Cognitive Behavioural Therapy procedures reduced depression among college students with high harm avoidance with depressive symptoms (Saigo, Hayashida, Tayama, Ogawa, Bernick, Takeoka, Shirabe, 2018).

I would like to reiterate here that research shows that harm avoidance is strongly associated with greater severity of suicide behaviour, though novelty seeking is also found to be associated with suicidality. This was observed independent of genetic factors. In simple terms harm-avoidance, the personality trait played a major role than genetic phenotypes. Researchers explained that Harm-avoidance involves anger-related problems (Perroud, et al.,2012).

Self-directedness

Self-directedness is a character dimension of personality assessment profiles. That is it is a unique attribute of one's personality (see definition of personality in the earlier part of this section on personality)

Self-directedness is

"the extent to which individuals are goal oriented and resourceful) (Gary VandenBos, 2015, p.g. 954).

According to Wikipedia,

"Self-directedness is a personality trait of self-determination, that is, the ability to regulate and adapt behavior to the demands of a situation in order to achieve personally chosen goals and values. It is one of the "character" dimensions in Cloninger's Temperament and Character Inventory (TCI). Cloninger has described it as "willpower", defined as "a metaphorical abstract concept to describe the extent to which a person identifies the imaginal self as an integrated, purposeful whole individual,

rather than a disorganized set of reactive impulses. (" Self-directedness, 2017, December 30).

This could be considered a protective factor against suicide. Research shows that individuals who had self-directedness have low suicidal behaviour (Woo, Jun, Jeon, Song, Kim, Kim et al. , 2014). Increase in self-directedness lowers depressive mood, especially suicide ideation (Lee, Lee, Kim, 2017). Self-directness also showed to be less found among suicide attempters (Calati, Giegling, Rujescu, Hartmann, Möller, De Ronchi, Serretti, 2008).

Since the above explanations might have been so boring that some may feel troublesome to read it. So I am summarizing this chapter in a picture form for your perusal.

Figure 3 Suicide Behavior from Individual perspective

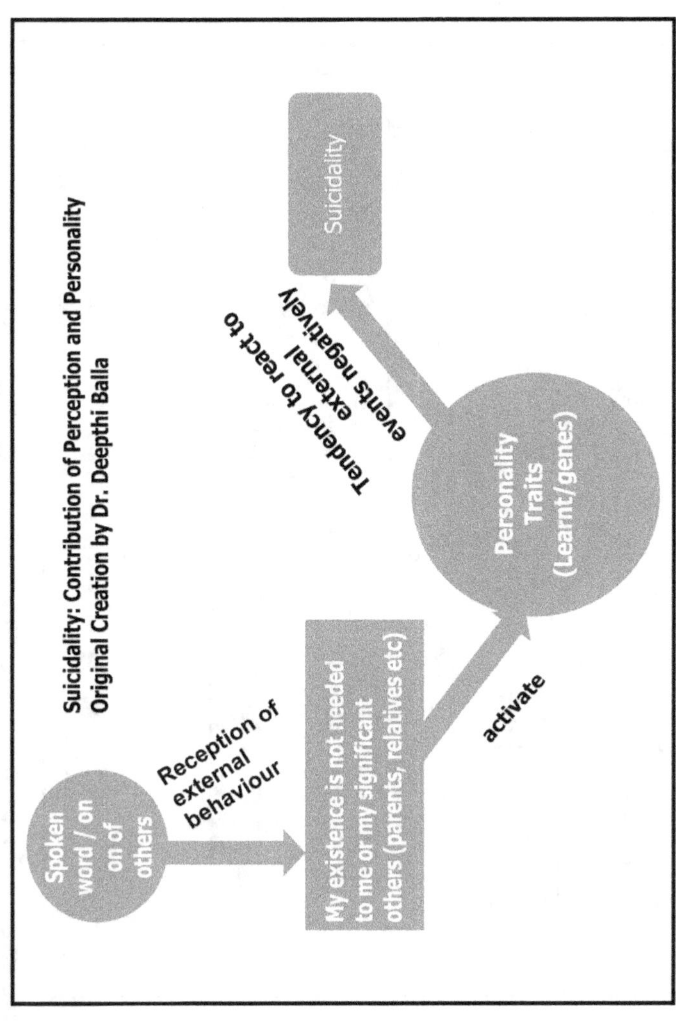

Since perception to suicide link was beautifully explained by Taylor's theory of suicide from Social Psychology perspective, I am leaving it untouched

Figure 4   Personality variables linked to suicide behaviour

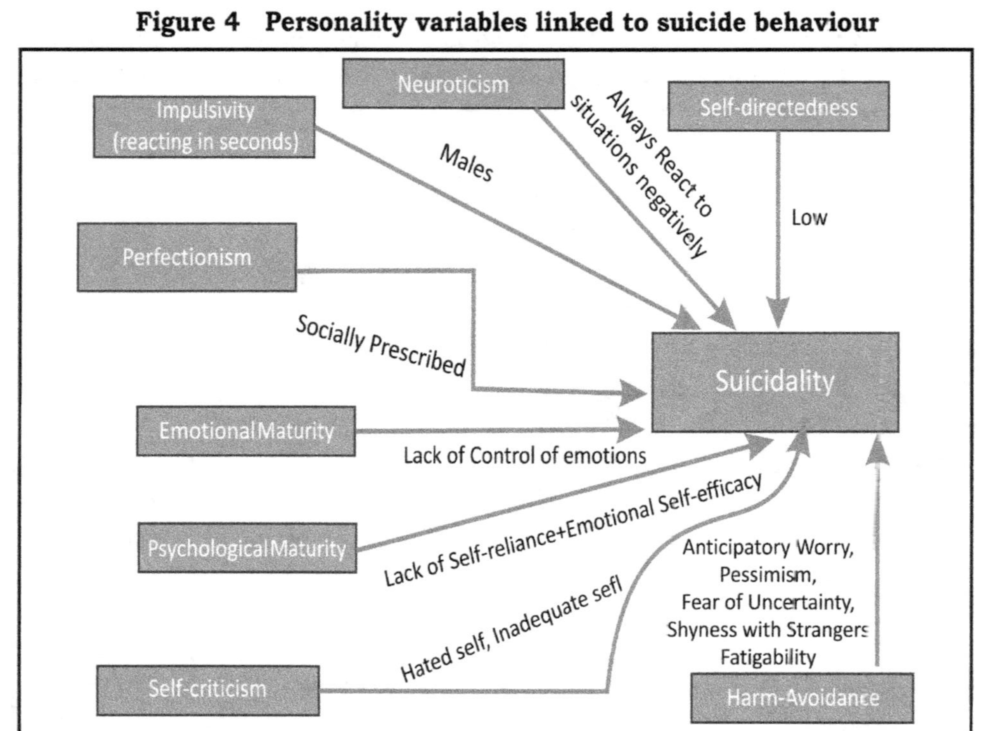

From the above two figures, I want the readers to understand that the traveller goes through a lot in terms of how he takes in the information from outside and how he reacts to the outside world.

Chapter 3

The Path

The path as per psychologists gets initiated in the minds of the suicidal individuals and is narrated at first by Sigmund Freud, who described the structure of mind (conscious, subconscious and unconscious), which almost majority of the public is aware of. Later on, many researchers pinpointed the psyche of suicidal and I am compiling their research findings, in a table format for quick understanding of their propagations.

J. Mark C. Williams and Leslie R. Pollock (2000); Israel Orbach (2003)., and E. David Klonsky, Alexis M. May, and Boaz Y. Saffer (2016) compiled books elaborating series of theoretical and experimental findings. I also compared it with O'Connor, Rory & Nock, Matthew. (2014) article on the psychology of suicidal behaviour.

I am explaining it in table form as described below.

Table 4- Description of psychological explanations of the suicidal psyche

Domain	Theorist/Researcher	Main propagation
Psychic	Sigmund Freud Freud	Suicide as the outcomeof the intra-psychic struggle. The struggle of dominance between psychic forces of life (libido-controlsunwanted / threatening experiences into the unconscious)and death (Thanatos).When Thanatos gains more power while libidinal energy depletes, a person commits suicide.
Affective	Zilboorg (1937)	Revenge, fear, spite and fantasies of escape are often the psychological triggers for suicide, most suicides are impulsive acts.
Affective	Menninger (1938)	3 psychological components of suicide ➤ The Wish to Kill ➤ The Wish to be Killed ➤ The Wish to Die
Affective	Litman (1967)	feelings of abandonment, helplessness and hopelessness, emotional states of guilt, rage, anxiety and dependency

Cognitive-affective	Sabbath (1969)	"expendable child" - childrenchildren interpret that their parents desire is to get "rid of him, for him to die"
Cognitive-Affective	Jacobs (1971)	Among the youth, Suicide is due to social isolation, which starts with family and then progresses to the society he is living in. No need for me in society. So gradually cuts all ties with the social units like family and others. Loneliness, alienation and lack social support.
Cognitive-Affective	Neuringer (1976)	Rigidity in thinking; not able to compromise when they feel that there are few opportunities in the life for relief or change.
Cognitive	Maris (1981)	Suicide is the result of 'suicide career', which depicts one's inabilityand unwillingness in coping with life difficulties. No compromise with life situations; so after repeated failures, the better (deciding for the whole life) coping strategy opted by the suicidal people is "suicide"

Affective	Shneidman's (1985)	Psychache-unbearable mental pain caused by "frustrated need". *"the suicidal person believes that their most important needs which define them as a unique person cannot be met and therefore the mental pain (shame, guilt, fear, anxiety, loneliness, angst, dread) will never cease, they will go on to commit suicide."*
Social factors	Orbach (1986,1988, 1989)	Suicide among young is due to familial situations and demands that pressure the child or adolescent to solve irresolvable problems.
Cognitive	Schotte and Clum (1987)	*"Cognitive vulnerability (eg, social problem solving) accounts for the association between stress and suicide risk".* It is known as Diathesis-stress- hopelessness model.
Affective	Duke and Lorch (1989)	low self-esteem correlated significantly in adolescents with suicidal intent and suicidal ideation
Affective	Baumeister (1990)	Suicide is due to the

		feeling of no escape from mental pain with the realization of one's failures and self-disappointments.
Affective	Linehan's (1993)	Suicide is due to 'emotional dysregulation *(inability to control emotions-either high or low).* Observable in children
		Emotional dysregulation is due to Biological predispositions (e.g.- personality traits that are inherited; determine how one spontaneously reacts to negative stimuli *invalidatingenvironments* an unsafe environment for children - e.g., child abuse
Cognitive	Williams, (1996); Goddard et al, (1996)	Depressed and suicidal individuals cannot solve problems as they arepoor at recollecting a strategy used for resolving similar problem successfullyfrom their specific memory in the past. So the only solution they think of is suicide.
Affective	Williams (1997)	a "cry of pain"; attempt

		to escape from the trapof the circumstances, feeling of being defeated (unemployment andclose relationships); inner turmoil; little likelihood of being rescued;
Cognitive	Mann and colleagues	Existence of a stressor i.e., a (1999) Psychiatric disease + how it is perceived + impulsivity
Cognitive-	Williams (2001)	*"Suicide risk is increased when affective feelings of defeat and entrapment are high and the potential for rescue (eg, social support) is low"*. Hence it is called Arrested flight model.
Cognitive	Joiner's (2005)	"interpersonal affective psychological theory of suicidal behaviour"; perception of *'thwarted belongingness and perceived burdensomeness.'* These result from the treatment of others toward one is not goodor the suicidal individual feel s not able to help for the welfare of close others. E.g.- peer rejection

Cognitive	Johnson and colleagues (2008); Wenzel and Beck (2008)	Suicidal risk can be perceived by andunderstanding "interplay between biases in information processing, schema, and appraisal systems"
Affective	(O'Connor 2011)	Integrated motivational-volitional theory Defeat and entrapment (facilitated by threat-to-self and motivational moderators)
Affective	(Klonsky & May 2015)	Three-step; Dispositional variable (genetic e.g.- pain sensitivity or blood phobia), Combined with the experience of pain and hopelessness, leads to suicidal behaviour especially when pain exceeds connectedness

From the above table, we can understand that there is a transition in the study of reasons for suicide, that started at considering suicide as a negative psychic force (Thanatos), emotional cry to interpersonal and social entrapment.

In addition to the psychological and emotional cries of the suicidal individual, there are some other physical and mental disorders which in the affected individuals lead to the path of suicide.

Bertolote, J. M., & Fleischmann, A. (2002) have presented interesting pictorial representation which notified of the comorbid psychiatric disorders found among suicide patients.

These researchers showed "Suicide and mental disorders: distribution of diagnoses in studies with *psychiatric inpatients*" in the following picture

Figure 5: Illustration of the percentage of suicide cases in psychiatric inpatients

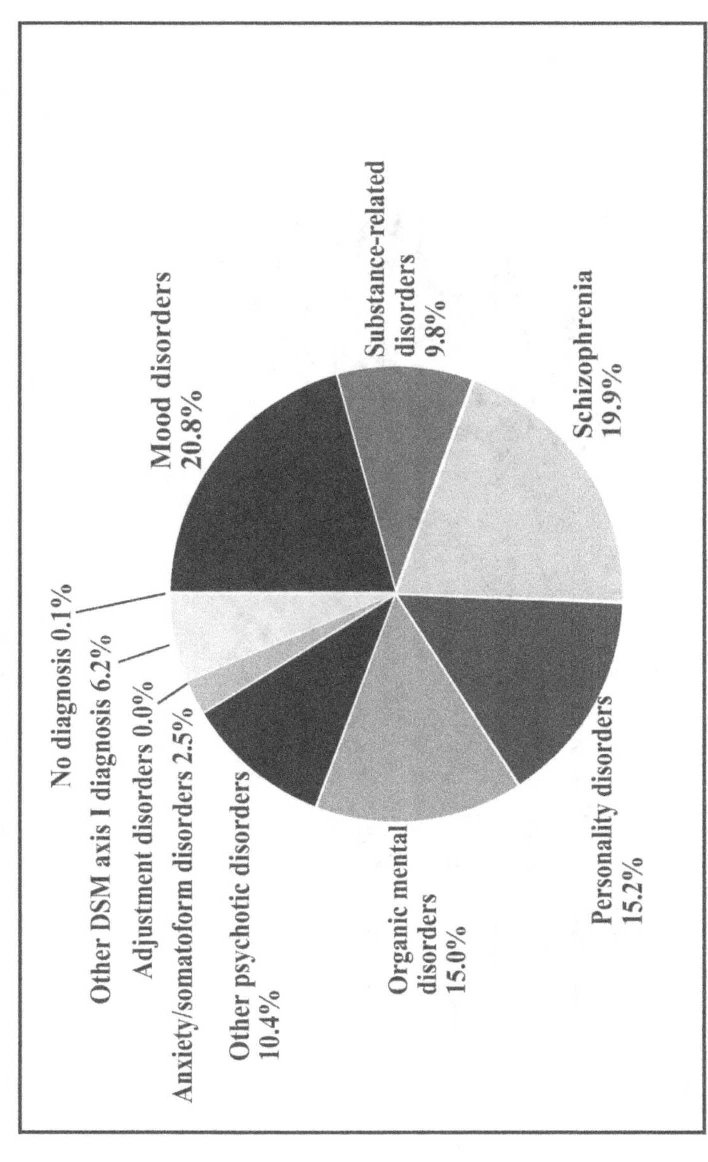

Figure - reused with the kind permission of Dr Bertolote, J. M.

Fig. 6: Illustration of the percentage of suicide cases in the General Population

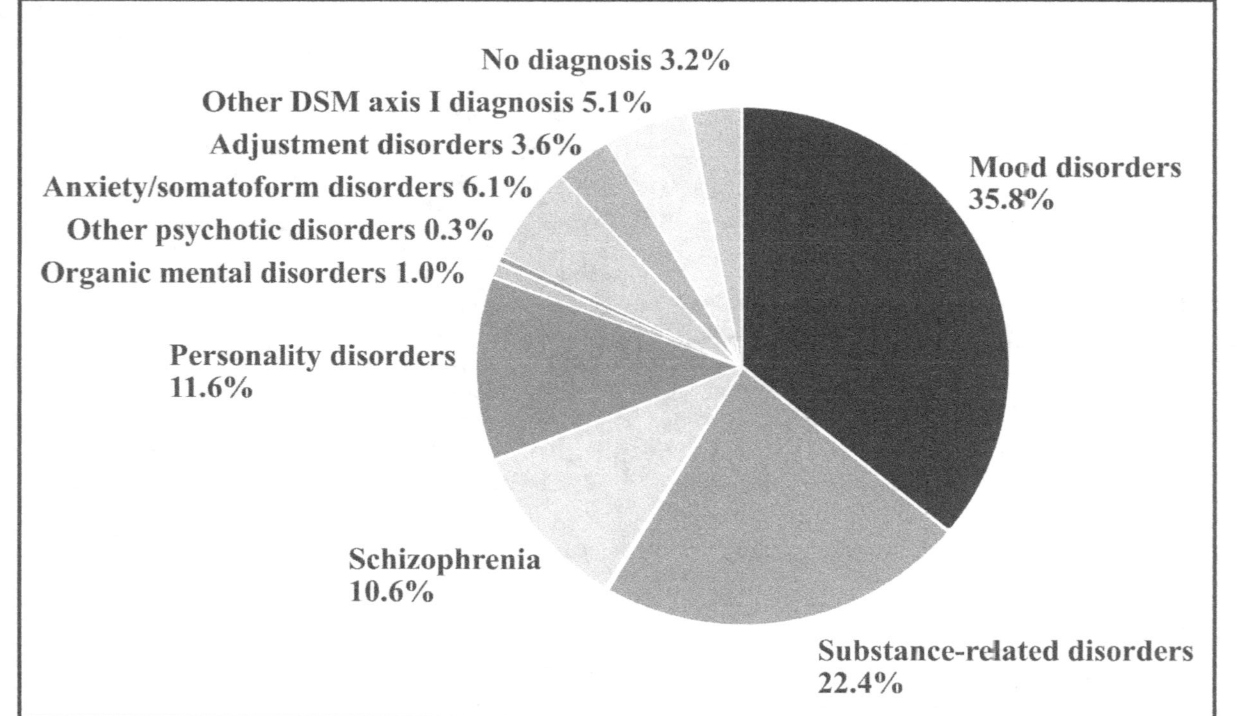

Figure - reused with the kind permission of Dr Bertolote, J. M.

Both these figures indicated that the percentage of mood disorders and its association to suicides in both psychiatric and general population is significant. Mood disorders in simple terms include mood variations where higher or escalated mood phenomenon like an excessive laugh, talking, irritation etc., are under the umbrella term mania (in clinical terminology manic episode) and the lower extreme of mood phenomena significantly known in the world as depression (Major Depressive Disorder, Depressive episode of bipolar disorders). Hence it is suggested that one should attend mental health clinics for a mental status check-up at least. I insist to all the readers who have some stigma that attending or visiting mental health clinics does not mean or indicate to the observers either to your relatives or social neighbourhood that, you are an insane person. I hope that as people in this modern age are cautious of dietary practices, so would also be cautious about mental well-being which could magnify your physical health practices such as diet balancing.

This link was explained by Epocrates an online athenahealthservice (2019), who pointed the British Journal of Psychiatry article of 1997 issue

Table 5: Expected Risk of Suicide in Psychiatric patients

	Risk for suicide with illness Vs. expected risk	Range
Child and adolescent psychiatric diagnoses	5 times greater	NA
Anorexia nervosa	23 times greater	0-100
Alcohol dependence and abuse	6 times greater	1-60
Opioid dependence and abuse	14 times greater	3-36
Sedative, hypnotic, or anxiolytic dependence	20 times greater Comorbid alcohol abuse (16x) Comorbid illicit drug abuse (44x)	NA
Mixed drug dependence and abuse	20 times greater	NA
Cannabis use	Relative risk among heavy users: 4 times greater vs. nonusers	NA
Schizophrenia	8.5 times greater	N/A
Major depressive disorder	20 times greater	0.8-115
Bipolar disorder	15 times greater	0-200
Dysthymia	12 times greater	0-133
Mood disorders not otherwise specified	16 times greater	4-38
Anxiety disorder	6 times greater	NA
Obsessive-compulsive disorder	10 times greater	NA
Panic disorder	10 times greater	0-37.5
Personality disorder	7 times greater	NA

Table6: Expected Risk of Suicide in Patients with Medical Illness

	Risk for suicide with illness vs. Expected link
Huntington disease	3 times greater
Epilepsy	5 times greater
Neurosurgery	20 times greater
Unspecified organic mental disorders	2 times greater
HIV/AIDS	7 times greater
Malignant neoplasms	1.8 times greater
Multiple sclerosis	2 times greater
Peptic ulcer	2 times greater
Renal disease - Hemodialysis and continuous ambulatory peritoneal dialysis	14 times greater
Spinal cord injury	4 times greater
Systemic lupus erythematosus	4 times greater

Comparison of risk for suicide with and without the presence of selected medical illnesses

Data adapted from Harris EC, et al. Br J Psychiatry 1997;170:205-228; McGirr A, et al. Journal of Clinical Psychiatry 2008;69:966-970; Harris EC, et al. Medicine (Baltimore) 1994;73:281-296; Anguiano LM. A literature review of suicide in cancer patients. Cancer Nursing. 2012;35:E14-E26.

Retrieved from: https://online.epocrates.com/diseases/101624/Suicide-risk-management/Etiology

The above table shows that suicide is found among "neurosurgery" and renal disease.

What are the motivators for the traveller to stick on to suicidal path?

As we looked into the above figures and tables, we perceived that certain disorders both physical and psychological to have strongly associated with suicidality in the affected individuals. But we cannot just brush off other attitudinal components which are insidious to suicidal behaviour formation and its development. This insidious behaviour makes the suicidal individual to only opt for suicide as the coping mechanism.

> Rumination

> Motivation-Implementation

Rumination

According to the Cambridge Dictionary of Psychology, Rumination is defined as - rumination n.

1. *Pondering or contemplating ideas or memories for a longer period than is normal. Excessive rumination is characteristic of obsessive-compulsive disorder.*

2. *The regurgitation, rechewing, and swallowing of food by grazing animals such as cows.*

3. *The regurgitation, rechewing, and swallowing or expectorating of food by humans, which is common among infants and profoundly retarded individuals and occurs occasionally in normal adults.*   *(David Matsumoto, 2009, p.g., 451)*

There are two types of rumination namely-brooding rumination and reflective rumination which had an association with suicide ideation.

Brooding Rumination

In the previous chapter, I have just defined brooding rumination, which makes the individual feel despair by comparing his present state of life with some unachieved or dissatisfied life event. It resonates in the mind of the person and makes him focus only on the negative life events rather than positive achievements. In psychiatric patients, it was noted that those with a history of suicide attempts have high brooding rumination and this strongly correlated with suicide attempts even after controlling current levels of depression. It means that more than depression, brooding rumination escalates the report of suicide attempts among psychiatric patients (Grassia, Marie & Gibb, Brandon, 2009).

Reflective Rumination

Reflective rumination is -

> *"labeled reflective pondering, involves attempts to understand the reasons for one's depressed mood."* (Miranda, & Nolen-Hoeksema, 2007).

Miranda R and Nolen-Hoeksema cited Treynor and colleagues (2003), who found that brooding predicted increases in depression while reflective pondering *predicted decreases in depression over one year (Miranda, & Nolen-Hoeksema, 2007).* It means that brooding focuses on why such bad events happened to one and reflective focuses on "why did such events occur?" Reflective tries to find out the solution or to be more precise tries to see what is wrong with one's emotional state of mind that makes one feel so helpless and hopeless. In the words of Miranda and Nolen-Hoeksema, brooding rumination predicts an increase in depression during the follow-up period. Whereas reflective rumination, is focusing on finding the origins of such feelings, predicted suicide ideation even at follow up period. In simple terms, the process of reflecting on 'what went wrong with me that I fell victim to such sorrow?" can sustain the suicide ideation until the individual can identify the source of distress correctly and get professional assistance in replacing these thoughts with positive memories and activities. Reflective rumination can predict suicide ideation even when depression and hopeless were kept constant among college students with prior suicide attempts (Surrence, Katherine & Miranda, Regina & Marroquín, Brett & Chan, Shirley, 2009). How can we identify whether someone is in rumination? One study showed that to maintain social bonds people tend to highlight one's flaws in a jovial context. This could make others lower their guard in the presence of this person who humiliated his 'self' to please them, and then facilitates a fresh start for the self-humiliating person, a relationship with this group (University of Granada, 2018, February 8). These self-humiliating jokes serve the purpose of managing or suppressing the anger of the speaker (Jorge Torres-Marín, Ginés Navarro-Carrillo, Hugo Carretero-Dios, 2018). Research shows that self-defeating humour style is strongly correlated with aggressive humour style (Leist, & Müller, 2013). But these humiliating jokes of the person, affects their future correspondence and leads to a ruminating style of thinking and finally makes one to become susceptible to suicide ideation. This is known as self-defeating humour. In particular, "greater use of a reflective ruminative style may lead to more usage of a self-defeating humor style which may, in turn, lead to higher levels of suicidal ideation (Tucker, Wingate, Slish, O'Keefe,

Cole, & Hollingsworth, 2014)." So as per the research self-defeating humour is an identifier of suicide ideation in long-term.

Examples would clarify this. Since it is subjective, I am taking the example given by wikiHow

> *I was complimented on my leather gloves the other day. I wasn't wearing any.*

> *I'm in shape. Round is a shape, right? ("Self Deprecating Humor Examples - wikiHow", 2019)*

In the first example, we see that the speaker is expressing her anger for the person who made the compliment. The complement addressed the speaker for what he or she is not wearing. The speaker perceived the complement is a sarcastic reminder that he or she should have worn the leather gloves. This when the speaker narrates, the listeners might take it as a joke. But the speaker felt humiliated when this happened to him or her. This is not related to suicide ideation in all situations. It depends upon the severity or value or level of hurt that the experienced person assumes to affect his or her worth of living. In my observations in my country, adolescent students have committed suicide for feeling humiliated for making them embarrassed in front of their classmates, especially opposite gender.

In the second example, the speaker is projecting his or her shape (physique) while taking care that the listeners would not take it seriously. But little focus is enough for any to perceive the dissatisfaction that the speaker has for his or her physique. There is a lot of research done on this issue which showed that negative body image is related to depression, anxiety and suicidality (Lifespan. 2006, June 6). Especially, an adolescent female had higher body dissatisfaction that is significantly correlated with low self-esteem and depression (Dilek Ozmen, Erol Ozmen, Dilek Ergin, Aynur Cakmakci Cetinkaya, Nesrin Sen, Pinar Erbay Dundar and Oryal Taskin, 2007). Whereas for an adult male, body dissatisfaction is correlated with social physique anxiety moderately (Schmidt, 2014)

It is not advisable to generalize that all those who use self-defeating humour have suicide ideation. But it gives you an idea that the individual has some conflict in his or her social relationships which is affecting his or her self-concept negatively. It could lead to frustration, stress, anxiety and depression. So it is advisable to suggest that if your child or beloved is manifesting self-defeating humour, approach him and make him(her) to get detoxified of such humour by initially talking to him (her) about such self-defeating humour and teach him that it is not magnifying what he or she is.

Motivation-Implementation

It Doesn't mean that those who ruminate would commit suicide. Unless the rumination triggers one of the basic motives of the individual it would not be turned into suicide ideation. Unless there is an item which is fatal to harm one's body is available to the individual action is not manifested. Dr.Thomas Joiner presented Inter Personal Theory of Suicide (IPT) wherein he emphasized that a suicide attempt is a complex process of three different feelings stemming from interpersonal conflicts. He meant that thwarted belongingness (e.g., 'I am alone") is not enough to make one attempt suicide. Similarly perceived burdensomeness (e.g.- " I am a burden") is not enough to make one attempt suicide. He also affirms that all those who could commit suicide will in reality commit suicide. Instead, he identified through his research that when all these three come to intersect with each other then only the desire to commit suicide turns into a lethal or near-lethal suicide attempt. Here near-lethal would be an NSSI attempt.

Fig 7. Model by Joiner T.E -why people die by suicide

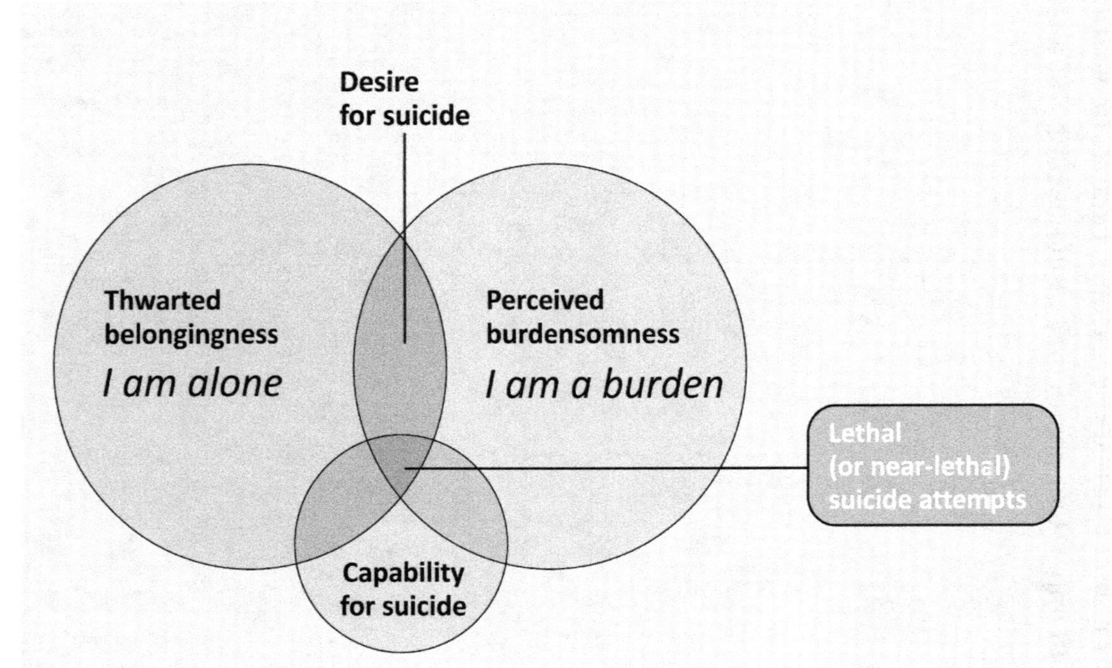

Joiner, T.E. (2005). Why people die by suicide. Cambridge, MA: Harvard University Press (in Press).

The above figure shows the entrapment of the suicidal who attempts suicide when the three aspects thwarted belongingness, perceive burdensomeness and capability for suicide come in contact in tune.

Furthermore, as an extension to Joiner's model, Klonsky, David & May, Alexis (2015) provided a decision tree to decide when to state that an individual has suicide ideation with a certain severity. He explained that it has 3 steps for the suicide ideation to transform into a suicide attempt.

Step-1: the individual is experiencing pain and hopelessness

> **PAIN + HOPELESS → SUICIDE IDEATION**

Step-2: the individual has suicide ideation and there are issues of pain and connectedness that cross the threshold

It means pain and connectedness either overcome each other to affect their level of suicide ideation.

> SUICIDE IDEATION + (PAIN < CONNECTEDNESS) → MODERATE SUICIDE IDEATION

> SUICIDE IDEATION + (PAIN > CONNECTEDNESS) → STRONG SUICIDE IDEATION

Klonsky, E David & May, Alexis (2015) pointed out that the existence of suicide ideation when coupled with a condition where pain either exceeds the connectedness or not, decides the level of severity of suicide ideation. Thus he ensures the importance of connectedness as a protective factor against suicide ideation. In simple words, we can understand that the feeling that we are in a supportive family, with supportive friends could alleviate the thoughts of suicide.

Step-3: With the presence of strong suicide ideation,

suicide attempts depend on the acquired capability to perform suicide act.

Klonsky, David & May, Alexis (2015) clarified that suicide attempts are possible when two processes get intermingled (mixed).

Those are -

➤   Acquired capability due to negative life events (suicide of family or friends etc), habituation to pain, physical abuse, NSSI etc

➤   Dispositional factors -i.e., genetics and pain sensitivity

This could be contemplated as followed-the situations make the strong suicide ideated person being unable to bear the events to decide upon suicide act as the only solution. But the vulnerability or susceptibility to suicide increases manifold in those strong suicide ideators with the above-mentioned experiences, when these have genetic components related to suicide, which act as fuel to the fire.

A more specific model of who will commit suicide was provided by O'Connor, Kirtley (2018) in their most influential work in suicidology to date -**"The Integrated Motivational-Volitional Model of Suicidal Behaviour"**

Figure 8 Model -The Integrated Motivational-Volitional Model of Suicidal Behaviour

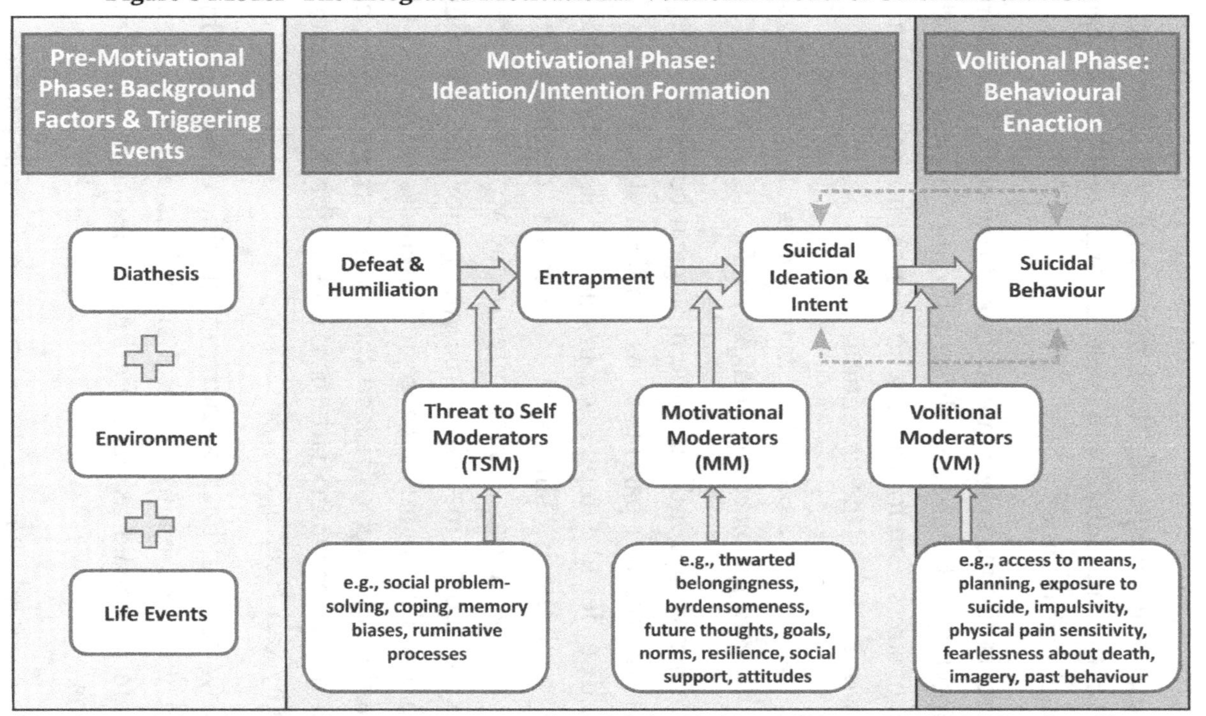

The above picture explains three phases of suicide behaviour. The first phase is the pre-motivational phase. The researchers explained that this involves background factors and triggering events. In specific these precipitate or initiate suicide thought in the individual with these factors. I will explain each in a simplified manner.

First is diathesis. When you look at the word, it is clearly understood by scholars and those who are familiar with the concept of stress. But for those who do not know the meaning of this word, here is the definition -

diathesis n. any susceptibility to or predisposition for a disease or disorder. ((VandenBos, 2015 p.g., 327)

Predisposition indicates the biological content which is transmitted from our parents to us. So if one has a history of a mood disorder like depression in one of the parents, it will become a diathesis. This is referred to as "diathesis-stress model" in psychological literature. In the words of Ingram and Luxton, (2005), in such people even minor stressors could ignite particular disorder (here it is depression). So the vulnerability or level of risk to the particular psychological disorder increases when diathesis is present for that disorder. (as cited by van Heeringen, 2012).

Now coming back to our model, this diathesis when coupled with the environmental situations and life events which are perceived as negative forms the basis for suicide ideations.

The second phase is the motivational phase, which the researchers' Prof Rory O'Connor and Dr Olivia Kirtley et al, (2018) referred to be the phase where the ideation or intention is formed. If you look at it closely it has some directional arrows indicating which leads to which. The first part ie., the defeat and humiliation gathered from the pre-motivational phase becomes fuel for this phase. It is like the CPU of the computer where the actual process of computing happens. Here the suicidal ideation is in the process of production. Like we add some ingredients in making a curry, so are some events that add a dark flavour making it impossible to have a positive thought to come out of suicide ideation. But the base ingredients are from the pre-motivational phase. The ingredients of the threat to self (see the picture for examples) meet the defeat to entrapment route in the middle making the route from defeat to entrapment a certain possibility. Entrapment is a very dangerous experience.

According to the free dictionary of Falex (online), the word entrap is defined as -

en·trap tr.v. en·trapped, en·trap·ping, en·traps

1.   To catch in or as if in a trap.

2.a.   To lure into danger, difficulty, or a compromising situation.

American Psychological Association Dictionary of Psychology defined entrapment as followed :

entrapment n. 1. a process in which one makes increasing commitments to a failing course of action or an unattainable goal in order to justify the amount of time and effort already invested, feeling helpless to do otherwise.

(VandenBos, 2015, p.g. 373)

The word entrap gives the idea that one is stuck in a swamp. Whereas the definition of American Psychological Association Dictionary of Psychology gives the idea that the person who is entrapped gives excuses for his present condition and why he is certain that he could not come out of the swamp. Now looking at IMV model, when the individual being in burdened by defeat also perceived threat to himself, quivers in fear and hopeless that none could save him. So this leads to entrapment where even a supporting hand could not be perceived by the entrapped person. This entrapments makes an individual think of human relationships in unsupportive and leads to the Motivational Moderators (MM). I encourage you to look at the figure of IMV model in this section. This according to O'Connor et al (2018) lead to suicide ideation.

The third phase 'Volition Phase' or 'Behavioral Enaction' involves a two-way interaction. I mean that suicide ideation of the motivation phase not only influences suicide behaviour but gets influenced by suicide behaviour in reciprocal. In a clear sense, it could be understood as we see that suicide attempters think about suicide frequently for successive trials in future. O'Connor, R.C., Kirtley, O.J. (2018) referred to factors that make it possible as 'Volitional Moderators (VM).' These researchers emphasize all the factors that make an individual commit suicide. For example accessibility to means (knife, rope, poison, sleeping pills etc), impulsivity, fearlessness et could make an individual take voluntary decision to commit suicide.

Hence it could be concluded that motivation plays an important role in suicide ideation. Combing Joiner (2005) and O'Connor, Kirtley, (2018) work, we must note -

> the background initiates negative environment within an individual,

> those which boost up these negative emotions, motivations and

> The means of self-harm should not be made available (considering the personality variables, pain sensitivity etc) to the suicidal

Hence I encourage the readers to be mindful of the issues discussed in this chapter while trying to judge a person who survived a suicide attempt.

Chapter 4

The Crossroads

So far we learned about the traveller and the path. That is what precisely makes the traveller have suicidal thoughts and what make him or her consider suicide as the only option. But does it mean that those who tread the path will reach the goal of ending one's life? No, certainly not. In many instances of biographical narrations, celebrities too experienced suicidal thoughts and wanted to kill themselves. But though they have attempted were fortunate to come out of it. They were fortunate enough to perceive and grab the opportunities that illuminated like the silver lining at the brim of the thick cloud.

Walt Disney, who invented and popularized our beloved cartoon Mickey Mouse too committed suicide when he was just 31 years old. But he was lucky enough to survive and in subsequent years developed Disney organization as we all know today ("21 Celebrities Who Narrowly Survived Suicide Attempts", n.d.). There are other celebrities like Mike Tyson, Princess Diana, Halle Berry, Elizabeth Taylor etc. as per the above source. But in every country celebrities are attempting suicides. It started when they are in their adolescence and but the common point to all is loneliness. They experienced the pain of not needed by their beloved. They felt they are betrayed. Their illusion of trusting people made them unable to cope with their betrayal and as it is a fatal blow to their emotional state, they have attempted suicide. But due to the support they received in the brink of suicide, they were able to come out of it successfully learning that blind trust on others is not profitable to themselves. Instead, they learned to trust and love themselves, keep oneself first and then to help others wisely (Lists, n.d.).

I entitled this chapter as 'the crossroads'. What are crossroads? It refers to be at an intersection point on the road where one can see many options or paths and is in a dilemma to choose between the existing. Here in the context of suicides, the individual decides to follow only one path that leads to suicide. There might have been different paths to follow. But my concern is why does the suicidal choose only that path which is dreadful?

After pondering on the crossroads imaginatively, I come up with the following as the core at the time of bubbling suicide thoughts.

1. Decision Making

2. Impulsive arousal at the moment

3. Existential Vacuum

1. Decision Making

Research suggests that suicide attempters who survived it, could not perceive the consequences of their actions in the light of the other available alternative options choosing which they might have avoided the suicide attempts. It takes a lot of time to make them understand that instead of carrying out suicide there are other options which are present at the moment of considering suicide (Dombrovski et al., 2018).

An interesting article in Chicago Tribune (2015) have cited the findings of Dr Fabrice Jollant, assistant professor of psychiatry at McGill University in Montreal. His observations are of value to understand what happens with the decision making of the suicide attempters.

Dr Fabrice Jollant points out that the suicide attempters :

➤ Risk takers

➤ Prefer short-term solutions over long-term solutions (immediate solutions)

➤ Unable to perceive alternative solutions

➤ Unable to control their thoughts

➤ Close relatives of suicide attempters show suicide vulnerable traits though are not exhibited

Dr Fabrice Jollant emphasizes that their inability to control their emotions could be a factor that is influencing their decision making and make them to choose death as the only option available to them.

To observe how suicide attempters perform decision making amidst a gambling or risk-taking situation, an experiment was conducted on suicide attempters (69 participants between 17-70 years age) of Europe. That is called IOWA Gambling task. These were presented with a task of choosing (clicking) 60 gambling cards that are displayed on the computer screen in 4 stacks. Some cards are meant to gain some profit and some cards will have a loss associated with them. Again some more cards in the stack are piled in such a way that choosing them will either give minimal loss or minimal gain. The suicide attempters (participants) have to click on the cards and if he or she clicks a card that is meant for success, he or she will either be rewarded with money or sometimes less money and for loss, there is no money being rewarded, which is only known to the experimenters. This uncertainty of gaining money or losing it seemed to affect violent suicide attempters to make more decision making mistakes gradually. Those of the participants who were nonviolent suicide attempters have exhibited emotional dysfunction (anger) in performing decision making task. Though the participants were not in a depressed mood at the time of testing, this decision making task can provoke emotional dysfunction. This impairment in decision making, according to the researchers reflected a neurological dysfunctioning observed in the orbitofrontal cortex area of the human brain. Thus the researchers concluded that -

'Impaired decision making, possibly due to emotional dysfunction, maybe a neuropsychological risk factor for suicidal behavior' (Fabrice Jollant et al., 2005).

2. Impulsive arousal at the moment

Often the decision to commit suicide is too short i.e., less than 5 minutes, which is observed to be the same in all suicidal incidents across different cultures ("Duration of Suicidal Crises", 2019).

Research showed that impulsive suicide attempters were younger in an age when compared to non-suicide attempters. Impulsive suicide attempters do not have any suicidal ideation or planning. They just act upon their impulse to commit suicide. Whereas non-impulsive suicide attempters were old people, single, widowed and divorced. These use lethal methods to commit suicide with planning. Non-impulsive suicide attempters had psychiatric symptoms as precipitators of their suicide attempts (Lim, Lee, & Park, 2016).

Impulsive suicide attempters exhibit the following characteristics:

1. Hopelessness but not depression

2. Leave clues to others that they are going to commit suicide

3. Involved in physical fights

Hence it is imperative to teach our youngsters to control their aggressive impulses so that impulsive suicide attempts could be predicted and preventable (R. Simon, Thomas & Swann, Alan & Kenneth Powell, & Potter, Lloyd & Kresnow, Marcie-jo & O'Carroll, Patrick, 2002). Thus it is recommended to engage these youngsters in fine arts, sports which will divert their aggressive impulses released, in the form of art that they are expressing.

One research showed that an important aspect of impulsiveness i.e., negative urgency -the reckless behaviour when one is in a negative mood state, seemed to be significantly associated with the planning of suicide attempts. It usually happens within the 12 hours of planning but is carried out in a minute due to the negative urgency one feels at the moment of peak negative affective state (Millner, Alexander Joseph, 2015).

3. Existential Vacuum

This term might seem new to many. But it has a lot of significance in suicide prevention. People who think of suicide often suffer from a lack of purpose. Thus when asked about why did they commit it, they would give an answer that they feel that there is no purpose in living. They would not be willing to be rescued. This turmoil was first recognized by Dr.Viktor Frankl an Austrian Neurologist and Psychiatrist. He had to work in a Nazi concentration camp during 1942-1945, during World War II time. He went there with his parents and wife but he is the only survivor of his family. He observed the soldiers who fought for the country and even have seen them losing the purpose of their lives. In subsequent years he wrote a book on "man's search for meaning."

("An Interesting Note on Suicide from Viktor Frankl - Jeffrey Alexander Martin - Medium", n.d.; "How Logotherapy Can Help You Find Meaning in Life", 2019)

What does this existential vacuum mean?

Dr Viktor Emil Frankl (1992) in his book "Man's search for Meaning" mentioned that

"Having shown the beneficial impact of meaning orientation, I turn to the detrimental influence of that feeling of which so many patients complain today, namely, the feeling of the total and ultimate meaninglessness of their lives. They lack the awareness of a meaning worth living for. They are haunted by the experience of their inner emptiness, a void within themselves; they are caught in that situation which I have called the "existential vacuum."(p.g., 48) "

"Not a few cases of suicide can be traced back to this existential vacuum. Such widespread phenomena as depression, aggression and addiction are not understandable unless we recognize the existential vacuum underlying them......For by filling the existential vacuum, the patient will be prevented from suffering further relapses. .(p.g.,49)"

As per the above passage, the main symptom of existential vacuum is -inner emptiness, lacking awareness of meaningfulness in one's life and is expressed through aggression, depression, suicides, and addiction.

Marshall Lewis a psychotherapist, logo therapist and existential analyst in his article concise Dr Viktor Frankl's concept of existential vacuum as followed.

> *"Frankl describes a person experiencing the existential vacuum as living in a world in which previous traditions and values no longer provide guidance on what to do and a world in which the person may not even know what she wishes to do. A person in this situation may then simply do what others do (conformism) or do what others tell her to do (totalitarianism). Manifestations of the existential vacuum include boredom, apathy, and sometimes noogenic neurosis, a clinical term devised by Frankl to describe psychological symptoms caused by moral and spiritual conflicts."*

The above observations made by Dr.Viktor Frankl infer the importance of considering "existential vacuum" when coming to treating depression. Both of these passages above describe that the person who is experiencing 'existential vacuum' as drained out of an individual's basic needs for existence. They simply reject that they exist in this world and their existence is of no value to themselves or others. So these wouldn't feel anything to contribute to the world. Dr Viktor Frankl's patients were mainly adults who visited psychiatric clinics. But if we look at the rates of depression among teenagers all over the world, we get alarmed. As per WHO it is more than 350 million. Much has been discussed about the prevention of suicides in research articles, but quite a few focused on the root symptom of this behaviour i.e., the suffering individual's "existential vacuum." Logo therapists and positive psychologists were the only professionals who addressed these components of existential vacuum in the process of attaining psychological wellbeing of an individual living in any society. For meaning and purpose in life are associated with the well-being of an individual as per positive psychology (Martin Seligman Ph.D., April 2011).

Ironically the people who search for their purpose of life are those who are experiencing an episode of depression or severely hurt to think of suicidal ideation.

"Suicidal ideation was significantly associated with major, spirituality level, connectedness, and meaning and purpose of life which explained 22% of variance in suicidal ideation (Choi, Soon-Ock; Kim, Sook-Nam, 2011)."

An explanation has been provided by Ewalds-Kvist, Lützén (2015) and Ewalds-Kvist, Béatrice & Lützén, Kim. (2015) observing two adults patients, who are suffering from ventilator-assisted tetraplegia. These researchers explained that

"life becomes existentially meaningful relative to inescapable suffering by the completion of three values: creative, experiential, and attitudinal values. If the search for meaning on these paths is frustrated or obstructed, a person's will to meaning transforms into existential frustration along with an existential vacuum and feelings of despair emerge and harm the person's will to survive."

This explained that the path, obstruction of which makes an individual commit harmful deeds.

From the work of Dr. Viktor Frankl, came a new branch

of psychotherapy called Logotherapy which tries to make the suicidal individual properly redefine the meaning of life. It is reported by Dr Ungar, a Logotherapist in logotherapy World Congress in Dallas that he observed a suicidal patient reluctant to get survive as the patient lost his meaning of living. The patient argued with the doctor about why he saved him. ("Meaninglessness and suicidal risk", 2011).

Meaningfulness is associated with lower depression symptoms (Kleftaras, George & Psarra, Evangelia, 2012). This is understandable that if one feels that he is living a meaningful life then he would not have time to get depressed but leads a life with contentment and true happiness.

By understanding existential vacuum that an individual feels, it could prove to be a great preventive measure against depression relapse and suicide behaviour (Robatmili, Somaye & Sohrabi, Faramarz & Ali Shahrak, Mohammad & Talepasand, Siavash & Nokani, Mostafa & Hasani, Mohaddese, 2014).

Now at the crossroads, when the person has already lost the will to live, would not accept any solution that is presented to him or her in any form. He would sacrifice his life in form of suicide, by choosing a destructive route. Though he survives one suicide attempt, he or she will try to commit again consecutively, unless the core feeling of not needed or meaninglessness of life be addressed. Thus there is a strong need to examine whether the suicidal person has lost meaning of life while treating him or her.

Thus I conclude this chapter saying that at the crossroad, suicidal will choose suicide path with decision-making impairment, impulsiveness at the moment and existential vacuum.

Chapter 5

The Highway

I entitled this chapter as a highway since highways connect one city to another city where there is a hope of obtaining the means that one seeks in that city. For example, an aspirant for Software Job, who is situated in a suburban or village in the states of India, mostly want to reach Bangalore as it is considered the IT hub. So they have some aspirations which will be met in the city of Bangalore. As a metaphor, we can observe here that the goal for these is straight forward and a mental highway is up to Bangalore though they will take any relevant transportation means like cars, bus, trains and Aeroplanes. Bangalore is the destination of their dreams. Here I used the term highway in the context of clear goal orientation. Similarly in the context of our journey, as long as one thinks of suicide he looks for ending the journey by looking at a path which ends with one's death. The suicidal doesn't care about what lies beyond the road he or she chooses. For the suicidal, he or she wants to end the conflict for which he or she doesn't seem to get the result that he or she desires. Thus I meant to create and show the barricades which will hide away the path of suicide to the suicidal. In psychological, mental health literature, these are known to be protective factors. But I want to go beyond the protective factors and try to contemplate all possible and simple solutions through which we can mask the road. Let us all find some ways through which in future we all can completely vanish the suicide road with a definitive way.

Highway in another sense, I meant to show you the

path that is broad and leads to a bright future. By showing this path, I want people to focus on larger issues, which demand your time so that there won't be time to think of short-cuts or by-pass routes to reach their desired goal, which could be fame, status or anything. Each of the celebrities we know Sylvestor Stalone, Ophra Winfrey, Michael Jordan and M.S.Dhoni etc., have to face struggles to reach their goal. Nothing comes easy to those who dream big. Those who dream big had to undergo constant struggle between their dreams (goals) and circumstances of life (reality) since our dreams are still in our hearts and imagination rather than in our physical setting, in specific in front of our eyes. Hear could happen in two situations. One is you overcome your circumstances by taking the help of others, you will reach your goal. Second is you get succumbed to your circumstances and your dream will forever seem to be lost. Let us imagine both of these as a see-saw where at one end is your dream and at the other end is your life circumstances. This would give you clarity. I encourage you to read the following link where I have seen the success stories of a few sports person, who motivated me.

The link is *https://blog.playo.co/10-inspiring-sports-stories-from-being-a-failure-to-success/*

1. Protective Factors

First of all, let us look at protective factors. In a simple sense, these are like sunscreen lotion which reflect the UV rays that fell on our body. These make an individual cope up with the stressful events which if not addressed could become serious mental wounds. So here we shall just look at protective factors against suicidal thoughts.

There are several systems which had their big role to play in making the individual fight suicide thought boldly. These encourage the individual to take a brave stance and fight it on his or her own. I am stressing here the point that "the individual fights on his own." It is the ultimate goal of counselling and psychotherapy to make an individual self-sufficient so that he (she) could survive on his (her) own without any scaffolding. So when an individual perceives that he had the support he needed or he has to support others (it is essential to have a belief that he is a must for the survival of others like kids and wife), he will gather the courage to look at the situation from another perspective. For instance, a single mother who after losing her husband might want to commit suicide, but the realization that she is enlightened to by the relatives who come to console her, makes her live strongly for her child. Until then her husband took care of economic issues like paying taxes, insurance etc., but now she had to take over those roles and responsibilities while not making the child aware of the struggles that she is facing every day. In India, many are at the bottom of their wish fulfilment conflicts but are sustaining everyday life with successfully avoiding committing suicide.

How is this possible? There is an answer which is in its culture, societal standards. The culture here stresses on family support, moral values and traditions which help in relieving their stress in forms of festivals. These aspects are observed all over the world. In particular, research showed some protective factors which are -survival and coping beliefs, the responsibility to family, and moral objections to suicide among Latinos (Oquendo, Maria & Dragatsi, Dianna & Harkavy-Friedman, Jill & Dervic, Kanita & Currier, Dianne & Keller Burke, Ainsley & Grunebaum, Michael & Mann (2005). Here moral objection to suicide is observed in a particular cultural group - Latinos. Similarly, each cultural group that exists in this world have some beliefs, which if used properly or magnified and transmitted to the next generation effectively, these suicide thoughts could be tackled easily. These beliefs will increase self-motivation and at the same time defensive wall against suicide provocations.

There is another line of research which revealed that there are gender differences in the ways that individuals fight against suicide. In specific, *'Focusing on positive among girls and self-discovery among boys* (Breton, Jean-Jacques & Labelle, Réal & Berthiaume, Claude & Royer, Chantal & St-Georges, Marie & Ricard, Dominique & Abadie, Pascale & Gerardin, Priscille & Cohen, David & Guilé, Jean-Marc., 2015)' found to be adoptive strategies against suicide. Among females there found to be an association between being female and low self-compassion. These have increased the manifestation of suicidality among female only (Chistopolskaya, Ksenia & Enikolopov, Sergey & Nikolaev, Evgeni & Drovosekov, Sergei., 2018). It means that the tendency of women who had low compassion for one's self had shown to have greater suicidal behaviour. In simple terms, we can understand that when a woman doesn't regard herself as needing self-compassion, there is a greater likelihood that she embraces risk as a coping mechanism. Just as we discussed in Chapter 2, all-or-nothing thinking plays its role at the time of suicide attempt.

Research also showed that **purposeful activities** that an individual engages himself in are definitive protective factors against suicide. These activities must be considered by the individual as purposeful. I mean that these are regarded as purposeful by the individual at a personal level. None should impose these activities on the individual. For instance, research showed that these activities include -'Traditional practices and subsistence activities, meaningful community involvement and an active lifestyle (DeCou, Christopher & Skewes, Monica & Lopez, Ellen., 2013).' From an observer point of view when I contemplated the above research finding, I am persuaded to put forth here the inference that, engaging in these activities makes the individual contributing something that one has by drawing it out from oneself and giving it to the needy who don't have it. Your inner voice shouts with joy saying "I served someone", "I had something valuable to help the needy." These altruistic acts elate one's self-concept. Simply one feels proud of oneself while engaging in such activities. This gives immense pleasure and shakes off the feelings of uselessness from the individual who had such negative self-evaluations about himself until then.

Presence of **Meaningfulness** in life and search for meaning mediated hopelessness and suicidality while these two suppressed *'negative disposition such as Negative Focus and Suicide Orientation (Lew, Bob & Chistopolskaya, Ksenia & Osman, Augustine*

& Huen, Jenny & Abu Talib, Mansor & Leung, Angel., 2020). What does it mean? Presence of meaningfulness indicates the enlightenment of meaningfulness either in one's childhood or at any early developmental stages that the individual gets so passionate about by the time he or she becomes adult. So the individual feels serving a purpose only when he engages in the activities which he or she is passionate about. Sometimes these passions lie dormant and suddenly triggered by an encounter with another individual, society or event. So engaging in these events pacifies the need for living with a purpose, which is essential every human being.

In some individuals, this meaningfulness is attained by observing and assimilating the meaningful activities of significant others like parents, relatives, friends, teachers and celebrities. In the extreme case of the example, we can observe fans of the movie stars participate in philanthropic activities that their favourite star exhibits in public. Like blood donation, alms-giving etc. are observed in such a scenario.

Meaningfulness determines the way one spends his daily life. It could make one understand why people develop maladaptive behaviours.

For example, see the following quote -

"When a person can't find a deep sense of meaning they distract themselves with pleasure" - by Viktor Frankl (Goodmorning Quote, 2018).

Here it should be noted that pleasure shouldn't be associated with physical/sensory needs but with leading life free of guilt. You can live boldly without fear of failure provided you achieved meaningfulness or at least in search of meaningfulness in life.

If teachers state such quotes in their class while modelling the same behaviour throughout the academic year in the school hours, children would, being witnessing it every day eventually imprint these attitudes for life long.

The major protective factor that could prevent a suicidal thought turning into a suicide attempt is **religiosity** (Burshtein, Dohrenwend, Levav, Itzhak & Werbeloff, & Davidson, Michael & Weiser, 2016).

I chose below a few definitions for explaining the term 'Religiosity.'

Oxford Advanced Learner's Dictionary states that religiosity refers to *"state of being religious or too religious' (Hornby, Albert Sydney., 2000)*

"extreme interest and belief in religion" ("RELIGIOSITY (noun) definition and synonyms | Macmillan Dictionary", 2020)

1.   *The quality of being religious.*

2.   *Excessive or affected piety.*

("Religiosity dictionary definition | religiosity defined", 2020)

These definitions indicate that religiosity refers to a person who has interest or beliefs in religion.

Many take it that both religiosity and spirituality are the same. But here I want to clarify the readers that these two are different. First I will show you the dictionary meaning and give you my observation of these two concepts.

Oxford Advanced Learner's Dictionary states Religion as-

"Noun 1[U] the belief in the existence of a god or gods, and the activities that are connected with the worship of them.

2 [C] one of the systems of faith that are based on the belief in the existence of particular god or gods. E.g.-Christianity, Islam and other world religions

2 [Sing.] a particular interest or influence that is very important in your life: For him, football is an absolute religion. (Hornby, Albert Sydney., 2000)"

Now coming to Spirituality Oxford Advanced Learner's Dictionary states -"the quality of being concerned with religion or human spirit" (Hornby, Albert Sydney., 2000)

The above definition of religion indicated that a person's belief in a God and working earnestly to appease the GOD, make a person considered a religious person. For example, giving alms to the poor as he took an oath to GOD that he will give alms to the poor if he does help him in a crisis. This is an extreme example. But sometimes parents inculcate the habit of being religious and the benefits of being religious are well taught in his early childhood. The external benefit is -gaining a good reputation in society that he is a religious man. The internal reward will be the peace of mind (especially superego is satisfied).

Whereas spirituality indicates a person's interest or inclination towards religion with the sole aim of finding one's spirit. Thus if one is devoting himself to meditation intending to attain the height of awareness of one's spirit and its connection with the supreme being then he is considered spiritual.

Through practising religion, the religious person has a

great support system which can be the "HOPE System" in times of facing crisis and chaos. The unexpected help that one gets in such times is what boosts their immunity. These do not worry much about what will happen in future if some catastrophe attacks them. Recently in a study conducted on nurses in China who are attending COVID-19 patients, the researchers found that while non-Muslims were afraid of death due to the fear of contamination of this mortally fatal disease, Islamic belief based Nurses expressed that they are not afraid because Allah will take care of them *(Jiang, Mengyao & Li, Siyan & She, Dongli & Yan, Fanghong & Chung, Yuet & Han, Lin., 2020)*

2. Defensive Mechanism

Defence Mechanism is a term well known to psychologists where one balancing structure of the mind, or the organizer of our mind, EGO uses several protective mechanisms which hide the problem the individual facing. Sometimes hiding the turmoil would make the individual maintain his serenity to protect his social self. Thus Ego uses denial, fantasy, sublimation, projection, identification etc. defence mechanisms to protect the balanced state of mind of an individual. But I am not talking about these. I meant to focus on shielding yourself from the outside effects or influences.

I put these in a separate heading, that there is a distinction between protective factors and defensive mechanisms. Protective factors are what makes an individual feel safe and at the time needs no or less effort to deal with the problems one faces. Whereas defensive mechanism is the efforts made by the individual to safeguard himself from incoming hazards.

For example, barricades are maintained by the soldiers to block the incoming attacks like bullets and bombs.

Now coming to suicide prevention, what defensive stances can you take?

1. Never give hold of your life to your emotions.

Emotions are very fragile, they can let you feel enraged or can even make you succumb to failure, neglect and rejection. Decisions taken under severe emotional pressure many times are found to be strong among suicide attempted individuals.

2. Respect your parents and Love yourself

Respecting our parents' decision regarding our safety, education, morals is a good practice, which helps us to learn from their experience. Respecting them is a form of love which we could show to them even when we are not in a position to repay their debt.

Now I mentioned above to love yourself. It doesn't mean to become self-lovers or narcissists. But it means that you must love your traits adequately. No low or No over the standards. Love your feature, your handwriting, your work and all you do with sincerity. By loving yourself properly, you will get new ideas on how to use your abilities, resources properly, when you are in crisis, provided you give time to focus on it for a few minutes. Those who love themselves adequately will also try to think differently about themselves. If someone insults you, then you will take it in another way -'they simply don't know what I am ".

3.Identify and exercise your character strengths and virtues to

flourish in life.

Virtues are the embodiment of different characters such as wisdom, justice, courage etc. These characteristics, each of us have, through proper analysis with the help of a Positive Psychologist, you can gain insight into what you are composed of. That means you will know what defines you. To recognize these character strengths lets you be self-confident and you will be able to project yourself efficiently in your social interactions.

Tyler, VanderWeele (2017) has explained the nature of flourishing as followed.

> *"Flourishing itself might be understood as a state in which all aspects of a person's life are good. We might also refer to such a state as complete human well-being."*

His statement declares that flourishing is to live with satisfaction in all spheres one's life.

He listed 6 factors like happiness and life satisfaction, mental and physical health, meaning and purpose, character and virtue, close social relationships, financial and Material stability.

After reading the above factors, one can sigh and feel -" is it possible to have all of these in one's life?" I am sure of it and can boldly say that not everyone will have all of them. But satisfaction is how one thinks or feels about issues of one's life. Job satisfaction related to how an employee feels about working in that organization in terms of how much the organization had a significantly positive effect on meeting his needs of life. If the salary is not sufficient to meet his needs of life like paying rent of his house, it will give him dissatisfaction. Moreover, if the working hours are increased without notice or added pay, then it will aggravate job dissatisfaction.

Then, how can one flourish? Flourish is the enlightenment of one's true potentials and utilizing them. Often we do not recognize our abilities which make us unique from others. In a simple sense, these are the tasks, which only you could do well in your family or among your peers. Notice them as long as you keep yourself absorbed in doing these, you will feel purposeful. When you feel purposeful then there will be less time to feel hopeless.

Research shows that flourishing is important for superior psychosocial functioning. Those who are deprived of this flourished state will fall into a state of languishing, which is indicated with symptoms of mental illness such as hopelessness. This languished state often leads to Major depressive disorder (Corey L.M.Keyes, 2002), one of its significant indicators is a suicide attempt.

4. Life is about creating and recreating goals to fulfil your purpose.

In life, we have different goals for different stages of life. When we are all kids, we have goals like passing an exam and reaching higher studies and then when we reached teenage our goal is to impress our peers' attention, freedom to do whatever one pleases; in adulthood the goal changes to much matured and most productive like marriage, rearing children, promotion in job, maintaining social status etc. For each gender these goals are different. We create goals either consciously or unconsciously, but these goals become our driving forces. In suicidal individuals, these goals seemed to be squashed by some uncontrollable event, person or thought. Unable to find a solution to come out of this situation, when adequate instruments are available (like a knife, rope or even a saree, overdosage of medicine), commit suicide.

Now the best possible solution for fighting against suicide thoughts is to check the goal which is trampled down or seems to be unattainable and then you can either modify it or completely replace it with another goal. For example, take a case of bullying in class. Suppose you got bullied in your class. The bullies are your classmates. Now the options that are available to you are like -talk to your class teacher in teacher's lounge or talk to your parents or try to transfer into the section if possible where these bullies are not found. You can change school in the worst scenario. If it produced dread in you, from which you are not able to come out easily, then you can opt for open schooling too. But you must consult parents first, then a counsellor.

5. Always be occupied with productive works like reading, painting/drawing, learning a new language, art, martial arts, planting seeds and taking care of them. So these will keep your mind active and will be less chance to fall into unnecessary emotions.

6. Learn to keep the "expectations" that you have about yourself and others have about you at a bay.

When I did my Ph.D., I asked intermediate college students (+2 or 11-12th grade) students what made them join the particular course. So I found that the expectations that the parents had for them lead them to develop depressive symptoms and suicidal ideation. Nearly 56 per cent have shown depressive symptoms due to the stress of academic self-expectations.

Just think normally, why do we do what we do now? I am writing this book because I wanted to. None pressurized me to do this. So I am doing it happily. But if there is pressure from someone and I am writing it not with my interest, then it will be a stressful event. If I let others keep on pressurizing me and write which I do not want to then at some point it creates stress and anxiety, which are harmful to both my body and mind. So I encourage you all to do what you love or modify the activity so that you will fall in love with the work that has been assigned to you.

With all these suggestions I close this book hoping that you would use all the information cited in this for yourselves and acquainted.

Epilogue

At the start of the book, I convinced you all that let us have an understanding of the concept of suicides. I hope I have made it clear to you all. It should be noted that suicide is not the product of an instant impulsive activity. That is to say, anyone except those with psychiatric disorders, would just get a spark and kill himself. For those who have never shown symptoms of depression but has committed suicide, there are many factors but the prominent one is hopelessness. I implore you all to be less judgmental about a suicide attempted individual. Circumstances which he lived in or he experienced might have made him think that there is no other option and there is no meaning for his survival in this world. Moreover, I heard some celebrities to over empathize with Mr Sushanth Singh's supposedly and alleged suicide and exclaimed that "he might have approached me", "he might have talked with me ." It puzzled me to hear such comments. The question that always roamed in my mind when I hear about such suicides is -What could lead him to commit it?   I go into a trance state and feel like I am in the victim's place or his family's place. I think of the conflict the individual has gone through. Why did he feel that none could help him? Do we also behave the same if we are in his place? How could we face if we are in his place? I request the readers to think of these questions in future when you hear about suicides.

All of us get depressed and even feel hopeless in our daily lives. I dare to state that each of our households has at least one individual who is depressed. Just remember about incidents of your life when you thought life is worthless but you can come out of it successfully without self-harm or harming others, who are around you at that time. So I implore you all not to be judgmental about suicidal individuals at the same time do not sympathize with them. Treat them as normal people and wait for the right moment to talk to them but talk naturally.

Since the primary cause of suicides is the feeling of hopelessness which is prolonged, this should be of much importance. Remember that you must see whether this hopelessness is not a feeling due to any medication that the individual is going through. Some medications for depression will have suicide provoking reactions within the body as one of the side effects. In such cases, you must approach your doctor from whom you are taking that medicine and explain your hopelessness feeling and the physical symptoms you observe while you are in that state.

Now if the hopelessness symptoms are pure of your emotional state consult a psychologist if available who will guide you with your emotional state and help you in understanding it properly and overcome that feeling adaptively. The Psychologist will also teach you some coping strategies and interventions which will benefit you in future too. If you have or someone whom you know attempts suicide frequently you must approach or advice the individual's family take him to a psychiatrist. Visiting a Psychiatrist for a consultation would not mean that you would get a tag of "insane" or mentally ill attached to your name. It will only be attached when you reveal this to untrustworthy people who know the matter.

Finally, I recommend all of us to habituate in engaging oneself always in purposeful activities and do feel meaningful. Meaningfulness can be experienced when you spend quiet time with the supreme being i.e., GOD every day. I assert this point here because our life is composed and surrounded by many uncontrollable forces. We cannot always cope-up with them. These will lead to hopelessness. People who have been diagnosed with a terminal illness like Cancer are also surviving with belief in GOD as it gives hope which thousands of inspirational books cannot give. This hope can bring miraculous changes in the immunity of the believers. This hope makes you live your present moment with happiness so that you can take steps with relaxation and thereby future will automatically be shaped Brightly. So I conclude it by stating this that Guard your lives with purpose and hope to enjoy the experiences of our Earth which is possible only with having healthy sensory organs of the body. If you commit suicide it is your wish, we cannot stop you. But remember these things. You will not have your body to experience the Earth again. You may say 'who needs to live in such a place.' Remember this world which seemed to you like that might be because of the encounters you had with worst kind of humans. But still, some good people are suffering the same as you. I saw many fan-made videos, and comments about Mr.Sushanth Singh Rajput and wished that he would know how many liked him. If he knew it, this might have been an energy booster for him. I stated here based on the assumption that his demise is due to Suicide. He is a brave man as per his body language. So please choose to live. If you don't want to live then do a field experiment of finding people who are suffering like you. Since you have decided to die there is no need for you to think about food, shelter, family etc. So go and survey them. It may give you new perspectives. I want you to gain experience firsthand rather than to depend on what others say to you like -"you don't know how fortunate you are to have a home, family etc." I state it because you cannot be able to listen to others' suggestions while you decided on suicide. Do this small experiment.

References

Preface

Bagla, Pallava (2014,Sept 4). "India Is Suicide Capital: World Health Organisation (WHO)." NDTV.com, Retrieved from, **https://www.ndtv.com/india-news/india-is-suicide-capital-world-health-organisation-who-659180**

David M. Fergusson; John Horwood L; Elizabeth M. Ridder; Annette L. Beautrais (2005). **Subthreshold Depression in Adolescence and Mental Health Outcomes in Adulthood.** Archives of General Psychiatry. Vol.62:66-72.

Hindustan Times, (New Delhi, 2018, Jun 01, 23:51 IST). Health ministry notifies Mental Healthcare Act 2017, attempting suicide no longer a crime in India. Retrieved from **https://www.hindustantimes.com/india-news/health-ministry-notifies-mental-healthcare-act-2017-attempting-suicide-no-longer-a-crime-in-india/story-yvvgLD3EOQ6mPWPSGLQyMO.html**

Niticentral (Sep 07, 2014). WHO report claims India is world's suicide capital. Retrieved on 1st Jan 2015 from **http://www.niticentral.com/2014/09/07/who-report-claims-india-is-worlds-suicide-capital-237412.html**

The Economic Times (2011, Jan 16). Every 4 minutes, one commits suicide in India. Economictimes.indiatimes.com. Retrieved September 28,2018 from: **//economictimes.indiatimes.com/articleshow/7297353.cms?utm_source=contentofinterest&utm_medium=text&utm_campaign=cppst**

The Week (New Delhi September 24, 2018 15:50 IST). Health experts call on government to form a national suicide prevention strategy "Suicide is not the solution and it is not wrong to ask for help". **www.week.in.** Retrieved September 28, 2018 from **https://www.theweek.in/news/sci-tech/2018/09/24/Health-experts-call-on-government-to-form-a-national-suicide-prevention-strategy.html**

Chapter1

Preparation for the Journey

AFSP. (2018). Risk Factors and Warning Signs. [online] Available at: https://afsp.org/about-suicide/risk-factors-and-warning-signs/ [Accessed 4 Oct. 2018].

American Psychiatric Association. (2013). Diagnostic and statistical manual of mental disorders (5th ed.).Pg.801,803-804. Arlington, VA: American Psychiatric Publishing.

Andreas Bähr (2013). Between "Self-Murder" and "Suicide": The Modern Etymology of Self-Killing. Journal of Social History, Volume 46, Issue 3, 1 Pages 620-632,**https://doi.org/10.1093/jsh/shs119.**

Andrew M. Colman (2nd ed.).(2006). Suicide. Oxford Dictionary Of Psychology. Oxford: Oxford University Press.

Andrew T. A. Cheng, Chau-Shoun Lee (2000). Suicide in Asia and the Far East. In Keith Hawton, Kees van Heeringen (Ed.) The International Handbook of Suicide and Attempted Suicide. (p.g.43-44). The Atrium, Southern Gate, Chichester, West Sussex PO19 SSQ, England. JOHN WILEY & SONS, LTD.,

Antoon A. Leenaars (2010). Edwin S. Shneidman on Suicide. Suicidology Online Vol.1:5-18.

Crossman, Ashley. (2018, September 29). The Study of Suicide by Emile Durkheim. Retrieved from **https://www.thoughtco.com/study-of-suicide-by-emile-durkheim-3026758**

https://www.etymonline.com/word/suicide

John Kalafat (2005). Suicide. In Thomas P.Gullotta, Gerals R.Adams. ED.).Handbook of Adolescent Behavioral Problems. Pg.232. Springer Science_Business Media, Inc., USA.

Noel Thomas(n.d). What does Durkheim's study suicide tell us about the role of social theory in his work more generally? (Retrieved from https://www.ivoryresearch.com/writers/noel-thomas-ivory-research-writer/ **https://www.ivoryresearch.com /writers/noel-thomas-ivory-research-writer/**

Chapter 2

The Lone Traveler

Andrew M. Colman (2nd ed.).(2006).Trait. *Oxford Dictionary Of Psychology.* Oxford: Oxford University Press.

Antoon A. Leenaars (2010). **Edwin S. Shneidman on Suicide.** Suicidology Online Vol.1:5-18.

Arezoo Shahnaz, Boaz Y. Saffer, E. David Klonsky (2018). **The relationship of perfectionism to suicide ideation and attempts in a large online sample.** *Personality and Individual Differences 130 :117-121. https:// doi.org/10.1016/j.paid. 2018.04.002*

Baetens, Imke & Claes, Laurence & Hasking, Penelope & Smits, Dirk & Grietens, Hans & Onghena, Patrick & Martin, Graham. (2013). **The Relationship Between Parental Expressed Emotions and Non-suicidal Self-injury: The Mediating Roles of Self-criticism and Depression.** Journal of Child and Family Studies. 24. 491-498. 10.1007/s10826-013-9861-8.

Baetens, Imke & Claes, Laurence & Hasking, Penelope & Smits, Dirk & Grietens, Hans & Onghena, Patrick & Martin, Graham. (2013). **The Relationship Between Parental Expressed Emotions and Non-suicidal Self-injury: The Mediating Roles of Self-criticism and Depression.** Journal of Child and Family Studies. 24. 491-498. 10.1007/s10826-013-9861-8.

Bo Bi*, Wei Liu, Die Zhou, Xu Fu, Xiaoxia Qin and Jiali Wu(2017). **Personality traits and suicide attempts with   and without psychiatric disorders: analysis of impulsivity and neuroticism.** *BMC Psychiatry. 17:294 DOI 10.1186/s12888-017-1453-5*

Brandon E. Gibb, Marie Grassia, Lindsey B. Stone, and Dorothy J. Uhrlass and John E. McGeary (2012). **Brooding Rumination and Risk for Depressive Disorders in Children of Depressed Mothers.** *Journal of Abnormal Child Psychology. 2012 Feb; 40(2): 317-326. doi: [10.1007/s10802-011-9554-y]*

Calati R, Giegling I, Rujescu D, Hartmann AM, Möller HJ, De Ronchi D, Serretti A(2008). Temperament and character of suicide attempters. *Journal of Psychiatric Research. Vol.42(11):938-45..DOI: 10.1016/j.jpsychires. 2007.10.006.*

Campos, Rui & Besser, Avi & Blatt, Sidney. (2013). **Recollections of Parental Rejection, Self-Criticism and Depression in Suicidality.** *Archives of suicide research : official journal of the International Academy for Suicide Research. 17.58-74.* 10.1080/13811118.2013.748416.

Campos, Rui & Holden, Ronald & Baleizão, Cristina & Caçador, Berta & Sofia Fragata, Ana. (2018). **Self-Criticism, Neediness, and Distress in the Prediction of Suicide Ideation: Results from Cross-Sectional and Longitudinal Studies.** *The Journal of Psychology. 152. 237-255. DOI : 10.1080/ 00223980.2018.1446895.*

Caroline Maskill and Dr Ian Hodges, Velma McClellan, Dr Sunny Collings (2005). Explaining Patterns of Suicide A selective review of studies examining social, economic, cultural and other population-level influences Report. Ministry of Health , PO Box 5013, Wellington, New Zealand. Retrieved from *https://www.health.govt.nz/system/files/documents/publications/ explainingpatternsofsuicide.pdf*

Castilho, Paula & Pinto-Gouveia, José & Duarte, Joana. (2016). Two forms of self-criticism mediate differently the shame-psychopathological symptoms link. *Psychology and Psychotherapy: Theory, Research and Practice. 90. 10.1111/papt.12094.*

Centre for Addiction and Mental Health. (2011, October 7). Genetic link to suicidal behavior confirmed. ScienceDaily. Retrieved July 26, 2020 from *www.sciencedaily.com/releases/2011/10/111007113941.htm*

Damian, L. E., Stoeber, J. Negru?Subtirica, O. and B?ban, A. (2017). On the Development of Perfectionism: The Longitudinal Role of Academic Achievement and Academic Efficacy. Journal of Personality, 85: 565-577. doi:10.1111/jopy.12261

David Matsumoto (Ed.) (2009). *Cambridge Dictionary of Psychology.* New York. Cambridge University Press.

Dr. Umesh Chandra Kapri and Dr. Neelam Rani (2014). Emotional Maturity: Characteristics and Levels. INTERNATIONAL JOURNAL OF

TECHNOLOGICAL   EXPLORATION   AND   LEARNING (IJTEL).Vol3(1):359-361.Retrieved from *https://ia600205.us.archive.org/18/ items/Httpijtel.orgv3n1359-361CRP0301P22.pdf/359-361CRP0301P22.pdf*

E. David Klonsky, Alexis M. May, and Boaz Y. Saffer (2016). Suicide, Suicide Attempts, and Suicidal Ideation. The Annual Review of Clinical Psychology. 12:307-30. doi:10.1146/annurev-clinpsy-021815-093204

Egress definition and meaning.[Def.2] Collins English Dictionary. (n.d.). Retrieved from https://www.collinsdictionary.com/dictionary/english/ egress

Elizabeth Landau (2009, March 24). Suicidal behavior may run in families. Retrieved on 26th July 2020 from *https://edition.cnn.com/2009/ HEALTH/03/24/suicide.hereditary. families/?iref=nextin*

Emotional Maturity. (2018). Retrieved from *http://psychology.wikia.com/ wiki/Emotional_maturity*

Falgares G, Marchetti D, Manna G, Musso P, Oasi O, Kopala-Sibley DC, De Santis S and Verrocchio MC (2018) **Childhood Maltreatment, Pathological Personality Dimensions, and Suicide Risk in Young Adults.** Frontiers in Psychology. 9:806. doi: 10.3389/fpsyg.2018.00806

Fazaa, Norman & Page, Stewart. (2003). Dependency and Self-Criticism as Predictors of Suicidal Behavior. Suicide & life-threatening behavior. 33. 172-85. 10.1521/suli.33.2.172.22777.

Flourish definition taken from https://dictionary. cambridge.org/ dictionary/english/flourish

Fry PS, Debats DL (2009). Perfectionism and the five-factor personality traits as predictors of mortality in older adults. *Journal of Health Psychology. Vol.14(4):513-24. doi: 10.1177/1359105309103571.*

Gau, Susan & Chen, Ying-Yeh & Tsai, Fang-Ju & Lee, Ming-Been & Chiu, Yen-Nan & Soong, Wei-Tsuen & Hwu, Hai-Gwo. (2010). **Risk Factors for Suicide in Taiwanese College Students.** *Journal of American college health : J of ACH. 57. 135-42. 10.3200/JACH.57.2.135-142.*

Gilbert, Paul & Clarke, M & Hempel, Susanne & Miles, Jeremy & Irons,

Chris. (2004). Criticizing and reassuring oneself: An exploration of forms, styles and reasons in female students. *The British journal of clinical psychology/ the British Psychological Society. 43. 31-50.10.1348/014466504772812959.*

Glassman, Lisa & Weierich, Mariann & Hooley, Jill & Deliberto, Tara & Nock, Matthew. (2007). Child Maltreatment, Non-Suicidal Self-Injury, and the Mediating Role of Self-Criticism. *Behaviour research and therapy. 45. 2483-90. 10.1016/j.brat.2007.04.002.*

Gong, Xiaopeng & Paulson, Sharon & Wang, Cen. (2016). Exploring family origins of perfectionism: The impact of interparental conflict and parenting behaviors. Personality and Individual Differences. 100. 43-48. 10.1016/j.paid.2016.02.010.

Hamid Khanipour, Mitra Hakim shooshtari and Reza Bidaki (2016). Suicide Probability in Adolescents With a History of Childhood Maltreatment: The Role of Non-Suicidal Self-Injury, Emotion Regulation Difficulties, and Forms of Self-Criticism. International Journal of High Risk Behaviors and Addictiction. 5(2):e23675. doi: 10.5812/ijhrba.23675.

Hewitt PL, Flett GL, Turnbull-Donovan W (1992). Perfectionism and suicide potential. The British Journal of Clinical Psychology.Vol.;31 (Pt 2):181-90.Retrieved from *https://www.ncbi.nlm.nih.gov/pubmed/1600402*

https://pdfs.semanticscholar.org/0ca5/ b31f39e453225c41ecf429a8f8f4c59b3db6.pdf.

J. Mark C. Williams and Leslie R. Pollock (2000). The Psychology of Suicidal Behaviour. In Keith Hawton, Kees van Heeringen (Ed.) The International Handbook of Suicide and Attempted Suicide. *(p.g.43-44).* The Atrium, Southern Gate, Chichester, West Sussex PO19 SSQ, England. *JOHN WILEY & SONS, LTD.,*

J. Mark C. Williams, Leslie R. Pollock (2000). The Psychology of Suicidal Behaviour. In Keith Hawton, Kees van Heeringen (Ed.) The International Handbook of Suicide and Attempted Suicide. (p.g.43-44). The Atrium, Southern Gate, Chichester, West Sussex PO19 SSQ, England. *JOHN WILEY & SONS, LTD.,*

Jarrett, C. (2017, July 27). Perfectionism as a risk factor for suicide - the most comprehensive test to date. Retrieved November 9, 2018, from *https:/ /digest.bps.org.uk/2017/07/27/perfectionism-as-a-risk-factor-for-suicide-the-most-*

comprehensive-test-to-date/

Jelena Brezo , Joel Paris, Richard Tremblay , Frank Vitaro (2006). Personality traits as correlates of suicide attempts and suicidal ideation in young adults. *Psychological Medicine. Vol. 36 (2) pp. 191-202. https://doi.org/ 10.1017/S0033291705006719*

Jess Fiest and Gregory Fiest(6th ed) (2006).Theories of Personality. Newyork : McGraw-Hill Companies, Inc.,

K.G.E. Sandquist, B.F.S. Grenyer & P. Caputi (2009). The Relation of Early Environmental Experience to Shame and SelfCriticism: Psychological Pathways to Depression. Proceedings of the 44th Annual APS Conference, pp. 161 - 16

Kiamanesh P, Dyregrov K, Haavind H, Dieserud G(2014) . Suicide and perfectionism: a psychological autopsy study of non-clinical suicides. *Omega (Westport). Vol.69(4):381-99. doi: 10.2190/OM.69.4.c.*

Kwon, S., & Weed, N. C. (2016, May 06). Neuroticism. Retrieved from https://www.britannica.com/science/neuroticism#accordion-article-history

Languish definition taken from https://en.oxforddictionaries.com/ definition/languish

Lee K, Lee HK, Kim SH (2017). Temperament and character profile of college students who have suicidal ideas or have attempted suicide. *Journal of Affective Disorders. Vol. 15;221:198-204. doi: 10.1016/j.jad.2017.06.025.*

Lence Milosevaa and Tatjana Vukosavljevic-Gvozden, (2014). Perfectionism Dimensions in Children: Association with Anxiety and Depression. *Procedia - Social and Behavioral Sciences 159 (2014) 78 - 81. doi: 10.1016/j.sbspro.2014.12.332*

Lessin DS, Pardo NT(2017). . The impact of perfectionism on anxiety and depression. Journal of Psychology and Cognition. Vol.2(1):78-82.Retrieved from *https://www.alliedacademies.org/articles/the-impact-of-perfectionism-on-anxiety-and-depression.pdf*

Liu, Shen-Ing & Huang, Yu-Hsin & Wu, Ying-Hui & Huang, Kuo-Yang & Huang, Hui-Chun & Sun, Fang-Ju & Huang, Chiu-Ron & Sung, Ming-Ru & Huang, Yo-Ping. (2017). Temperament traits in suicidal and non-suicidal mood disorder patients in Taiwan. *Psychiatry Research. 253. 260-266. 10.1016/*

j.psychres.2017.04.003.

Liya Panayotova (Mar 27, 2016). Types of Self-Criticism. Retrieved Nov 21, 2018 from Explorable.com: https://explorable.com/e/types-of-self-criticism

Marc Baertschi, Alessandra Costanza , Alessandra Canuto and Kerstin Weber (2018). The Function of Personality in Suicidal Ideation from the Perspective of the Interpersonal-Psychological Theory of Suicide. *International Journal of Environmental Research and Public Health. 15, 636; doi:10.3390/ijerph15040636*

Martin M. Smith, et al (2018). The perniciousness of perfectionism: A meta-analytic review of the perfectionism-suicide relationship. Journal of Personality. Vol.86:522-542. DOI: 10.1111/jopy.12333

Meerae Lim, Soojung Lee and Jong-Ik Park (2016). Differences between Impulsive and Non-Impulsive Suicide Attempts among Individuals Treated in Emergency Rooms of South Korea. Psychiatry Investigation Vol. 13(4):389-396. DOI: https://doi.org/10.4306/pi.2016.13.4.389

Mehmet YUMRU, Haluk A. SAVAS, Hasan HERKEN, M. Hanifi KOKACYA (2009). Suicide and Personality. Psikiyatride Guncel Yaklasimlar. Anatolian Journal of Psychiatry 2008; 9:232-237. https://www.researchgate.net/publication/38100989_Suicide_and_Personality

Morales-Vives, Fabia & Dueñas, Jorge Manuel. (2018). Predicting Suicidal Ideation in Adolescent Boys and Girls: The Role of Psychological Maturity, Personality Traits, Depression and Life Satisfaction. *The Spanish Journal of Psychology. 21. 10.1017/sjp.2018.12.*

O'Connor, Rory & Noyce, Rosie. (2008). Personality and cognitive processes: Self-criticism and different types of rumination as predictors of suicidal ideation. *Behaviour research and therapy. 46. 392-401. 10.1016/j.brat.2008.01.007.*

Paul Gilbert, Mark W.Baldwin, Chris Irons, Jodene R.Baccus and Michelle Palmer (2006).Self-criticism self-warmth: An imagery study exploring their relation to depression. *Journal of Cognitive Psychotherapy: An International Quarterly.Pg.,183-200.Retrieved from https://compassionatemind.co.uk/uploads/files/self-criticism-and-self-warmthjcp.pdf*

Paul L. Hewitt, Carmen F. Caelian Chang Chen and Gordon L. Flett, (2014). Perfectionism, Stress, Daily Hassles, Hopelessness, and Suicide Potential in Depressed Psychiatric Adolescents. *Journal of Psychopathology and Behavioral Assessment · DOI: 10.1007/s10862-014-9427-0*

Pennel L, Quesada JL, Dematteis M (2018). Neuroticism and anxious attachment as potential vulnerability factors of repeat suicide attempts. *Psychiatry Research. Vol.264:46-53. DOI: 10.1016/j.psychres.2018.03.064. Epub 2018 Mar 27.*

Perroud, N., et al., (2012). Temperament personality profiles in suicidal behaviour: An investigation of associated demographic, clinical and genetic factors. *Journal of Affective Disorders. in suicidal behaviour: 146(2).* http://dx.doi.org/10.1016/j.jad.2012.09.012

Peters, E., John, A., Bowen, R., Baetz, M., & Balbuena, L. (2018). Neuroticism and suicide in a general population cohort: Results from the UK Biobank Project. BJPsych Open, 4(2), 62-68. doi:10.1192/bjo.2017.12

Prof Paul Gilbert (n.d.). Compassion Focused Therapy Self-Criticism. Retrieved 23rd Nov 2018 from https://contextualscience.org/files/CFT%20ACBS%20Sevilla% 202017%20Part%20Three.pdf

Pychyl, T. A. (2008, April 30). What Flavor of Perfectionist Are You? It Matters! Retrieved from https://www.psychologytoday.com/us/blog/dont-delay/200804/what-flavor-perfectionist-are-you-it-matters

Rachael Wyatt , Paul Gilbert (1998). Dimensions of perfectionism: A study exploring their relationship with perceived social rank and status. *Personality and Individual Differences. Volume 24, Issue 1, Pages 71-79. https://doi.org/10.1016/S0191-8869(97)00146-3*

Raffaella Calati , Ina Giegling , Dan Rujescu , Annette M. Hartmann , Hans-Ju¨rgen Mo¨ller , Diana De Ronchi , Alessandro Serretti (2008). *Temperament and character of suicide attempters. Journal of Psychiatric Research 42 (2008) 938-945. DOI: 10.1016/j.jpsychires.2007.10.006*

Rappaport LM, Flint J, Kendler KS (2017). Clarifying the role of neuroticism in suicidal ideation and suicide attempt among women with major depressive disorder. *Psychological Medicine. Vol. 47(13):2334-2344. doi: 10.1017/S003329171700085X.*

Robert A.Baron, (2001). Psychology. New Delhi. Prentice-Hall of India Private Limited.

Rodzi?ski P1, Rutkowski K1, Soba?ski JA1, Mielim?ka M1, et al, 2015). Changes in neurotic personality profile associated with reduction of suicidal ideation in patients who underwent psychotherapy in the day hospital for the treatment of neurotic and behavioral disorders. **Psychiatria Polska. Vol.49(6):1323-41. doi: 10.12740/PP/OnlineFirst/37308.**

Roxborough HM, Hewitt PL, Kaldas J, Flett GL, Caelian CM, Sherry S, Sherry DL (2012). Perfectionistic self-presentation, socially prescribed perfectionism, and suicide in youth: a test of the perfectionism social disconnection model. *Suicide & Life-Threatening Behavior. Vol. 42(2):217-33. doi: 10.1111/j.1943-278X.2012.00084.x.*

Rui C. Campos, Ronald R. Holden, Cristina Baleizão, Berta Caçador & Ana Sofia Fragata (2018) Self-Criticism, Neediness, and Distress in the Prediction of Suicide Ideation:Results from Cross-Sectional and Longitudinal Studies. *The Journal of Psychology, 152:4, 237-255, DOI: 10.1080/ 00223980.2018.1446895*

S.K.Mangal, (2002). Advanced Educational Psychology. What is Personality?New Delhi. Prentice-Hall of India Private Limited.

Sabry M. Abd-El-Fattah , Hessa Abdulrahman Fakhroo(2012). The Relationship among Paternal Psychological Control and Adolescents' Perfectionism and Self-Esteem: A Partial Least Squares Path Analysis. *Psychology. Vol.3, No.5, 428-439. http://dx.doi.org/10.4236/psych.2012.35061*

Saigo T, Hayashida M, Tayama J, Ogawa S, Bernick P, Takeoka A, Shirabe S (2018). Prevention of depression in first-year university students with high harm avoidance: Evaluation of the effects of group cognitive behavioral therapy at 1-year follow-up. Medicine (Baltimore). *Vol. 97(44):e13009. doi: 10.1097/ MD.0000000000013009.*

Santhi Periasamy and Jeffrey S. Ashby (2002). Multidimensional Perfectionism and Locus of Control. Journal of College Student Psychotherapy 17(2):75-86. DOI: 10.1300/J035v17n02_06.

Self-directedness. (2017, December 30). Retrieved from https:// en.wikipedia.org/wiki/Self-directedness

Singh PK, Rao VR (2018). Explaining suicide attempt with personality traits of aggression and impulsivity in a high risk tribal population of India. PLoS ONE 13(2): e0192969. *https://doi.org/10.1371/journal.pone.0192969*

Soenens, Bart & Luyckx, Koen & Vansteenkiste, Maarten & Luyten, Patrick & Duriez, Bart & Goossens, Luc. (2008). Maladaptive Perfectionism as an Intervening Variable Between Psychological Control and Adolescent Depressive Symptoms: A Three-Wave Longitudinal Study. Journal of family psychology : JFP : journal of the Division of Family Psychology of the American Psychological Association (Division 43). 22. 465-74. 10.1037/0893-3200.22.3.465.

Suicidepreventioncommunity.files.wordpress.com.(2018).[online] available at https://suicidepreventioncommunity.files. wordpress.com/2009/03/shneidman_10-commonalities.pdf [accessed 5, October 2018]

Turkheimer, E. (2018). The Nature-Nurture Question. [online] Noba. Available at: https://nobaproject.com/modules/the-nature-nurture-question [Accessed 4 Oct. 2018].

Valois, Robert & J. Zullig, Keith & A. Hunter, Amy. (2013). Association Between Adolescent Suicide Ideation, Suicide Attempts and Emotional Self-Efficacy. *Journal of Child and Family Studies. 24. 10.1007/s10826-013-9829-8.*

Woo YS, Jun T-Y, Jeon Y-H, Song HR, Kim T-S, Kim J-B, et al. (2014) Relationship of Temperament and Character in Remitted Depressed Patients with Suicidal Ideation and Suicide Attempts-Results from the CRESCEND Study. *PLoS ONE 9(10): e105860. https://doi.org/10.1371/journal.pone.0105860*

Xavier, Ana & Pinto-Gouveia, José & Cunha, Marina. (2016). Non-suicidal Self-Injury in Adolescence: The Role of Shame, Self-Criticism and Fear of Self-Compassion. *Child & Youth Care Forum. 45. 10.1007/s10566-016-9346-1.*

Zai CC, de Luca V, Strauss J, et al(2012). Genetic Factors and Suicidal Behavior. In: Dwivedi Y, editor. The Neurobiological Basis of Suicide (Chapter 11 :pp1-3). Boca Raton (FL): CRC Press/Taylor & Francis; Available from: https://www.ncbi.nlm.nih.gov/books/NBK107191/

Zai, Clement & Manchia, Mirko & de Luca, Vincenzo & Tiwari, Arun & Chowdhury, Nabilah & Zai, Gwyneth & Tong, Ryan & Yilmaz, Zeynep & Shaikh, Sajid & Straus, John & Kennedy, James. (2011). The brain-derived neurotrophic factor gene in suicidal behaviour:A meta-analysis. The international journal of neuropsychopharmacology/official scientific journal of the Collegium Internationale Neuropsychopharmacologicum (CINP). 15. 1037-42. 10.1017/S1461145711001313.

Zhang, Huaiyu & N. Watson-Singleton, Natalie & E. Pollard, Sara & Pittman, Delishia & Lamis, Dorian & L. Fischer, Nicole & Patterson, Bobbi & J. Kaslow, Nadine. (2017). Self-Criticism and Depressive Symptoms: Mediating Role of Self-Compassion. OMEGA - Journal of Death and Dying. 003022281772960. 10.1177/0030222817729609.

Chapter 3

The Path

Bertolote, J. M., & Fleischmann, A. (2002). Suicide and psychiatric diagnosis: a worldwide perspective. *World psychiatry : official journal of the World Psychiatric Association (WPA), 1(3), 181-5.Retrived from https:// www.ncbi.nlm.nih.gov/pmc/articles/PMC1489848*

David Matsumoto (Ed.) (2009). Cambridge Dictionary of Psychology. New York. Cambridge University Press.

Dilek Ozmen, Erol Ozmen, Dilek Ergin, Aynur Cakmakci Cetinkaya, Nesrin Sen, Pinar Erbay Dundar and E Oryal Taskin (2007). The association of self-esteem, depression and body satisfaction with obesity among Turkish adolescents. BMC Public Health. 7:80. Doi: https://doi.org/10.1186/1471-2458-7-80

Entrapment(n.d).Retrievedfromhttps://www.thefreedictionary.com/entrapment

Online.epocrates.com. (2019). Suicide risk management etiology - epocrates online. [online] available at: https://online.epocrates.com/diseases/101624/suicide-risk-management/etiology [accessed 15 jan. 2019].

Grassia, Marie & Gibb, Brandon. (2009). Rumination and Lifetime History of Suicide Attempts. International Journal of Cognitive Therapy - *International Journal Of Cognitive Therapy. Vol.2(4): 400-406. DOI :10.1521/ijct.2009.2.4.400.*

Israel Orbach (2003). Suicide prevention for adolescents.In Robert A. King, Alan Apter(Ed.,). Suicide in Children and Adolescents P.g.228. Cambridge University Press The Pitt Building, Trumpington Street, Cambridge, United Kingdom.

J. Mark C. Williams and Leslie R. Pollock (2000). The Psychology of Suicidal Behaviour. In Keith Hawton, Kees van Heeringen (Ed.) The International Handbook of Suicide and Attempted Suicide. *(p.g.43-44). The Atrium, Southern Gate, Chichester, West Sussex PO19 SSQ, England. JOHN WILEY & SONS, LTD.,*

Joiner, T.E. (2005). Why people die by suicide. Cambridge, MA: Harvard University Press.

Jorge Torres-Marín, Ginés Navarro-Carrillo, Hugo Carretero-Dios (2018). Is the use of humor associated with anger management? The assessment of individual differences in humor styles in Spain. *Personality and Individual Differences Volume 120. Pages 193-201. https://doi.org/10.1016/j.paid.2017.08.040.*

Klonsky, E David & May, Alexis. (2015). The Three-Step Theory (3ST): A New Theory of Suicide Rooted in the " Ideation-to-Action " Framework. *International Journal of Cognitive Therapy. Vol.8(2). 114-129. DOI: 10.1521/ijct.2015.8.2.114.*

Leist, A.K. & Müller, D. (2013). Humor Types Show Different Patterns of Self-Regulation, Self-Esteem, and Well-Being. Journal of Happiness Studies. Vol. 14(2) : 551-569. https://doi.org/10.1007/s10902-012-9342-6

Lifespan. (2006, June 6). Negative Body Image Related To Depression, Anxiety And Suicidality. ScienceDaily. Retrieved June 9, 2019 from www.sciencedaily.com/releases/2006/06/060606224541.htm

Miranda, R., & Nolen-Hoeksema, S. (2007). Brooding and reflection: rumination predicts suicidal ideation at 1-year follow-up in a community sample. *Behaviour research and therapy, 45(12), 3088-3095. doi:10.1016/ j.brat.2007.07.015*

O'Connor, R.C., Kirtley, O.J. (2018). The Integrated Motivational-Volitional Model of Suicidal Behaviour. *Philosophical Transactions of the Royal Society B. 373: 20170268. DOI: 10.1098/rstb.2017.0268*

O'Connor, Rory & Nock, Matthew. (2014). The psychology of suicidal behaviour. *The Lancet Psychiatry. Vol.1(1): 73-85. Doi: 10.1016/S2215-0366(14)70222-6.*

Schmidt,, Z. (2014). Contingent self-worth and social physique anxiety as predictors of body dissatisfaction in young adult men. Retrieved from https://pdfs.semanticscholar.org/db26/248a33b10dc73955a86da2d6e441f199f7c2.pdf

Self Deprecating Humor Examples - wikiHow. (2019). Retrieved from https://www.wikihow.com/Sample/Self-Deprecating-Humor

Surrence, Katherine & Miranda, Regina & Marroquín, Brett & Chan, Shirley. (2009). Brooding and reflective rumination among suicide attempters: *Cognitive vulnerability to suicidal ideation. Behaviour research and therapy. 47(9): 803-8. DOI: 10.1016/j.brat.2009.06.001.*

Tucker, R. P., Wingate, L.R. R., Slish, M. L., O'Keefe, V. M., Cole, A. B., & Hollingsworth, D. W. (2014). Rumination, Suicidal Ideation, and the Mediating Effect of Self-Defeating Humor. *Europe's Journal of Psychology, 10(3), 492-504. doi:10.5964/ejop.v10i3.758*

University of Granada. (2018, February 8). Self-defeating humor promotes psychological well-being, study reveals. ScienceDaily. Retrieved June 7, 2019 from *www.sciencedaily.com/releases/2018/02/180208104225.htm*

van Heeringen K (2012). Stress-Diathesis Model of Suicidal Behavior. In: Dwivedi Y, editor. The Neurobiological Basis of Suicide. Boca Raton (FL): CRC Press/Taylor & Francis; Chapter 6. Available from: https://www.ncbi.nlm.nih.gov/books/NBK107203/

VandenBos, G. (2015). APA dictionary of psychology (2nd ed., pp. 327,373). Washington, DC: American Psychological Association.

Chapter 4

The Crossroads

21 Celebrities Who Narrowly Survived Suicide Attempts. Retrieved from https://www.suggest.com/celebs/4797/21-celebrities-who-narrowly-survived-suicide-attempts/

An Interesting Note on Suicide from Viktor Frankl - Jeffrey Alexander Martin - Medium. Retrieved from https://medium.com/@jeffreyalexandermartin/an-interesting-note-on-suicide-from-viktor-frankl-229b5dfae08f

Chicago Tribune (2015). Retrieved from https://www.chicagotribune.com/lifestyles/health/sc-hlth-0827-what-leads-to-suicide-20150827-story.html

Choi, Soon-Ock; Kim, Sook-Nam;(2011). Suicidal Ideation and Spirituality of College Students. The Journal of Korean Academic Society of Nursing Education. *Volume 17, Issue 2, 2011, pp.190-199. DOI : 10.5977/JKASNE.2011.17.2.190*

Dombrovski AY et al., (2018). Value-based choice, contingency learning and suicidal behavior in mid-life and late-life depression. Biological Psychiatry [e-pub]. (https://doi.org/10.1016/j.biopsych.2018.10.006)

Duration of Suicidal Crises. (2019). Retrieved from https://www.hsph.harvard.edu/means-matter/means-matter/duration/

Ewalds-Kvist B, Lützén K(2015).Miss B Pursues Death and Miss P Life in the Light of V. E. Frankl's Existential Analysis/Logotherapy. Omega (Westport). 2015;71(2):169-97. http://www.ncbi.nlm.nih.gov/pubmed/26625511

Ewalds-Kvist, s. Béatrice & Lützén, Kim. (2015). Miss B Pursues Death and Miss P Life in the Light of V. E. Frankl's Existential Analysis/Logotherapy. *OMEGA--Journal of Death and Dying. 71(2): 169-196. DOI :*

10.1177/0030222815570599.

Fabrice Jollant MS et al., (2005). Impaired Decision Making in Suicide Attempters. *The American Journal of Psychiatry. Vol.162(2).Pg.304-310. https://doi.org/10.1176/appi.ajp.162.2.304*

How Logotherapy Can Help You Find Meaning in Life. (2019). Retrieved from https://www.verywellmind.com/an-overview-of-victor-frankl-s-logotherapy-4159308

Kleftaras, George & Psarra, Evangelia. (2012). Meaning in Life, Psychological Well-Being and Depressive Symptomatology: A Comparative Study. *Psychology. 03(4). Pg. 337-345.DOI:10.4236/psych.2012.34048.*

Lim, M., Lee, S., & Park, J. I. (2016). Differences between Impulsive and Non-Impulsive Suicide Attempts among Individuals Treated in Emergency Rooms of South Korea. *Psychiatry investigation, 13(4), 389-396. doi:10.4306/pi.2016. 13.4.389*

Lists, C. Celebrities Who Attempted Suicide. Retrieved from https://www.ranker.com/list/celebrities-who-attempted-suicide/celebrity-lists

Marshall H. Lewis(n.d). The Existential Vacuum. Accessed at http://www.marshallhlewis.net/LTEAOnline/Vacuum.pdf

Martin Seligman Ph.D., (April 2011). The Original Theory: Authentic Happiness. Retrieved form https://www.authentichappiness.sas.upenn.edu/learn/wellbeing

Meaninglessness and suicidal risk. (2011). Retrieved from https://meaningtherapy.wordpress.com/2011/07/10/meaninglessness-and-suicidal-risk/

Millner, Alexander Joseph. (2015). Clarifying the Pathway to Suicide: An Examination of Subtypes of Suicidal Behavior and Their Association With Impulsiveness.. Doctoral dissertation, Harvard University, Graduate School of Arts & Sciences. http://nrs.harvard.edu/urn-3:HUL.InstRepos: 23845414. Retrieved from https://dash.harvard.edu/handle/1/23845414?show=full

R. Simon PhD, Thomas & Swann, Alan & Kenneth E. Powell MD, MPH & Potter, Lloyd & Kresnow, Marcie-jo & O'Carroll, Patrick. (2002). Characteristics of Impulsive Suicide Attempts and Attempters. *Suicide and Life-Threatening Behavior. 32. 49 - 59. 10.1521/suli.32.1.5.49.24212.*

Robatmili, Somaye & Sohrabi, Faramarz & Ali Shahrak, Mohammad & Talepasand, Siavash & Nokani, Mostafa & Hasani, Mohaddese. (2014). The Effect of Group Logotherapy on Meaning in Life and Depression Levels of Iranian Students. *International Journal for the Advancement of Counselling.*

37. 54-62. 10.1007/s10447-014-9225-0.

Viktor E. Frankl (4th Ed.,) (1992). Man's Search for Meaning: An Introduction To Logotherapy. Beacon Press 25 Beacon Street, Boston, Massachusetts.

Chapter 5

The Highway

Breton, Jean-Jacques & Labelle, Réal & Berthiaume, Claude & Royer, Chantal & St-Georges, Marie & Ricard, Dominique & Abadie, Pascale & Gerardin, Priscille & Cohen, David & Guilé, Jean-Marc. (2015). Protective Factors Against Depression and Suicidal Behaviour in Adolescence. *Canadian journal of psychiatry. Revue canadienne de psychiatrie. 60(2). S5-S15.*

Burshtein, S & P Dohrenwend, B & Levav, Itzhak & Werbeloff, N & Davidson, Michael & Weiser, M. (2016). Religiosity as a protective factor against suicidal behaviour. *Acta psychiatrica Scandinavica. 133(6). DOI: 10.1111/ acps.12555.*

Chistopolskaya, Ksenia & Enikolopov, Sergey & Nikolaev, Evgeni & Drovosekov, Sergei. (2018). Self-compassion as a protective factor against suicidal behavior: evidence for interplay with gender.

Corey L.M.Keyes (2002). The Mental Health Continuum: From Languishing to Flourishing in Life. Journal of Health and Social Research. *Vol. 43: 207-222. Retrieved on 5th July 2020 from http://midus.wisc.edu/findings/ pdfs/56.pdf*

Goodmorning Quote, (2018). 26 Deep Meaningful Quotes about Life with Images. Good Morning Quote. Retrieved 21 March 2020, from https:/ /www.goodmorningquote.com/meaningful-quotes-life/.

Hornby, Albert Sydney. (2000). Oxford advanced learner's dictionary of current English / [by] A.S. Hornby ; editor Sally Wehmeier. Oxford, England :Oxford University Press,

Lew, Bob & Chistopolskaya, Ksenia & Osman, Augustine & Huen, Jenny & Abu Talib, Mansor & Leung, Angel. (2020). Meaning in life as a protective factor against suicidal tendencies in Chinese University students. BMC Psychiatry. 20. 10.1186/s12888-020-02485-4.

Oquendo, Maria & Dragatsi, Dianna & Harkavy-Friedman, Jill & Dervic, Kanita & Currier, Dianne & Keller Burke, Ainsley & Grunebaum, Michael & Mann, J. (2005). Protective Factors Against Suicidal Behavior in Latinos. *The Journal of nervous and mental disease. - Vol. 193(7) - p 438-443. 193. 438-43. DOI: 10.1097/*

01.nmd.0000168262.06163.31.

R. DeCou, Christopher & Skewes, Monica & Lopez, Ellen. (2013). Traditional living and cultural ways as protective factors against suicide: Perceptions of Alaska Native university students. *International journal of circumpolar health. 72. 10.3402/ijch.v72i0.20968.*

RELIGIOSITY (noun) definition and synonyms | Macmillan Dictionary. Macmillandictionary.com. (2020). Retrieved 21 March 2020, from *https://www.macmillandictionary.com/dictionary/british/religiosity.*

Religiosity dictionary definition | religiosity defined. Yourdictionary.com. (2020). Retrieved 21 March 2020, from https://www.yourdictionary.com/religiosity.

Tyler J. VanderWeele (2017). On the promotion of human flourishing. PNAS Vol.114 (31): 8148-8156; *https://doi.org/10.1073/pnas.1702996114.*

About the Author

Dr Deepthi Balla (B.Sc., M.Ed., M.A.(Psy), PhD) is a UGC JRF and Lectureship qualified, who did her PhD on "reasons for depression and suicide ideation among Intermediate College students of Visakhapatnam." She has worked as a JRF in Andhra University for 2 years and has 1 and half year experience of teaching M.Sc., Psychology students. Her specializations are Educational Psychology, Health Psychology, Social Psychology and especially Adolescent Mental Health. Her work is published in the Times of India 2013 Newspaper. When her PhD is declared she got appreciation and she was interviewed in several State News Channels such as Tv9 (6-01-2015). She wrote articles on depression and suicide ideation in several journals and magazines. She is trained in Suicide Ideation Assessment and interventions by the American Psychological Association.

She is an International Affiliate Member of the American Psychological Association, Life Associate member of Indian Association of Clinical Psychology and National Positive Psychology Association. In addition to these, she acquired a top 1% in the NPTEL Positive Psychology program conducted by SWAYAM. She also qualified in Introduction to Japanese Language and Culture.

She had undergone resilience training from a renowned Doctor and Resilience Practitioner of UK in 2017 and then Positive Psychology program in 2018. She is a certified Cogmed Coach. Since 2018 she has been working as a guest faculty in Visakha Govt. Degree & P.G college for women teaching Psychology to MSc Psychology Students.